Harcourt

Math

Grade 4

ISBN 978-0-544-26822-7

 4 5 6 7 8 9 10   0982   22 21 20 19 18 17 16 15

4500520493   B C D E F G

Core Skills Math

GRADE 4

Table of Contents

© Houghton Mifflin Harcourt Publishing Company

Table of Contents

Core Skills Math, Grade 4

Common Core State Standards for Mathematics Correlation Chart

Operations and Algebraic Thinking

Use the four operations with whole numbers to solve problems.

4.OA.1	33
4.OA.2	34, 71, 72, 73
4.OA.3	39, 144, 145, 146, 147, 148, 149, 150, 151, 152, 153

Gain familiarity with factors and multiples.

4.OA.4	15, 16, 28, 29, 30, 31, 32

Generate and analyze patterns.

4.OA.5	139, 140, 141, 142, 143

Number and Operations in Base Ten

Generalize place value understanding for multi-digit whole numbers.

4.NBT.1	7, 8
4.NBT.2	1, 2, 5, 6, 9, 10, 11
4.NBT.3 _Supporting Skills_	12, 13, 14 3, 4

Use place value understanding and properties of operations to perform multi-digit arithmetic.

4.NBT.4	17, 18, 19, 20, 21, 22, 23, 24, 25, 26, 27
4.NBT.5	50, 51, 52, 53, 54, 55, 56, 57, 58
4.NBT.6	35, 36, 37, 38, 74, 75, 76, 77

Number and Operations—Fractions

Extend understanding of fraction equivalence and ordering.

4.NF.1	103, 104
4.NF.2 _Supporting Skills_	105, 106, 107, 108 122

Build fractions from unit fractions by applying and extending previous understandings of operations on whole numbers.

4.NF.3	
4.NF.3.a	115, 117, 119, 120
4.NF.3.b	110, 111

4.NF.3.c		121, 123, 124
	Supporting Skills	109
4.NF.3.d		114, 116, 118, 125
4.NF.4		
4.NF.4.a		112
4.NF.4.b		101, 102, 113, 126
4.NF.4.c		127, 128
Understand decimal notation for fractions, and compare decimal fractions.		
4.NF.5		137, 138
4.NF.6		131, 132, 133, 134, 135
4.NF.7		136

Measurement and Data

Solve problems involving measurement and conversion of measurements from a larger unit to a smaller unit.		
4.MD.1		45, 59, 60, 62, 63, 65, 66, 67, 68, 69
	Supporting Skills	61, 64
4.MD.2		40, 41, 42, 43, 44, 46, 47, 48, 49, 70
4.MD.3		92, 93, 94, 95, 96
Represent and interpret data.		
4.MD.4		129
Geometric measurement: understand concepts of angle and measure angles.		
4.MD.5		
4.MD.5.a		130
4.MD.5.b		100
4.MD.6		83, 84
4.MD.7		85, 86

Geometry

Draw and identify lines and angles, and classify shapes by properties of their lines and angles.	
4.G.1	78, 79, 80, 81, 82, 87
4.G.2	97, 98, 99
4.G.3	88, 89, 90, 91

Expressing Numbers

Express each number in two other ways.

1. $10,000 + 600 + 7$

   _____

   _____

2. ninety thousand, five hundred

   _____

   _____

3. 34,060

   _____

   _____

4. $7,000 + 800 + 60 + 4$

   _____

   _____

MIXED APPLICATIONS

5. The longest river in the United States is the Mississippi River. It is 2,348 miles long. Write the number in words.

   _____

   _____

6. The longest river in China is the Yangtze. It is three thousand, nine hundred fifteen miles long. Write the number in standard form.

   _____

   _____

NUMBER SENSE

Think of place-value blocks (ones, tens, hundreds, and thousands). Write the number and kind of blocks you could use for each of the following.

7. Show 7,020 using only tens. _____

8. Show 11,100 using only hundreds. _____

9. Show 231 using the same number of tens and ones. _____

10. Show 12,132 using the same number of thousands, tens, and ones.

   _____

Exploring Place Value

Write each number in standard form in the place-value chart.

THOUSANDS	HUNDREDS	TENS	ONES

1. eighty-seven

2. four hundred thirty-two

3. nine hundred five

4. four thousand, seven hundred seven

5. six thousand, twenty-four

6. seven thousand, one hundred forty-five

7. two thousand, one

MIXED APPLICATIONS

8. Mr. Taylor gets a check for one thousand, four hundred twenty-seven dollars. How would the amount be written in standard form?

   _____

9. Sue earns eight hundred forty-three dollars a week. Ken earns seven hundred eighty-nine dollars a week. Who earns more?

   _____

10. Ms. Huang's monthly pay is $2,045. This month she is given a $1,000 bonus. What is her monthly pay this month?

    _____

LOGICAL REASONING

Choose the best answer. Circle a, b, c, or d.

11. There are about _____ pages in your math book.

    a. 2   **b.** 20   **c.** 200   **d.** 2,000

Place Value to Hundred Thousands

Write the value of the digit 4 in each number in two other ways.

1. 3,456

2. 48,062

3. 59,241

4. 497,216

_____   _____   _____   _____

_____   _____   _____   _____

Write the value of the underlined digit in two other ways.

5. 4<u>3</u>7,215

6. 96,3<u>0</u>7

7. 48,<u>1</u>62

8. <u>9</u>76,002

_____   _____   _____   _____

_____   _____   _____   _____

9. Express the number eight hundred fourteen thousand, two hundred six in two other ways.

_____   _____

MIXED APPLICATIONS

10. How many zeros must you write beside the digit 4 to show a value of forty thousand? Write the number of zeros and write the number in standard form.

_____

11. Two hundred eighty-nine thousand, three hundred people live in Newton. Write the number in standard form and expanded form.

_____

_____

LOGICAL REASONING

12. Enter the number 186,275 into a calculator. You can change the 6 to 0 using one operation—subtracting 6,000. All the other digits remain the same. Tell how you can make these changes in one operation.

a. change 8 to a 4 _____

b. change 7 to a 9 _____

Place Value to Millions

Name the place value shown by the underlined digits.

1. 1,667,495 _____

2. 657,604,980 _____

3. 258,418,732 _____

Write the number that is 1,000,000 more.

4. 67,016,018 _____

5. 639,540,086 _____

Write the number that is 10,000,000 less.

6. 23,579,410 _____

7. 845,270,100 _____

MIXED APPLICATIONS

Study the number in the box. Write *true* or *false*.

> 18 million, 6 hundred

8. The standard form is 18,600. _____

9. The expanded form is 10,000,000 + 8,000,000 + 600 _____

10. The digit in the thousands place is 6. _____

11. The value of the digit in the hundred-thousands place is 0. _____

LOGICAL REASONING

12. In a secret code, a letter stands for each digit from 0 to 9. Use the clues to complete the code.

    Clues:

    a. ABH < DBH   D = _____

    b. DJ > DC   C = _____

CODE	
A = 7	B = 3
C = ?	D = ?
E = 5	F = 4
G = 0	H = 9
I = 6	J = 2

Forms of Numbers

Write two other forms for each number.

1. 102,060 _____

2. five hundred sixty-three thousand, four hundred _____

3. 300,000 + 80,000 + 900 + 60 + 2 _____

_____

Write the value of each underlined digit in two ways.

4. 129,<u>4</u>15 _____

5. <u>5</u>61,204 _____

MIXED APPLICATIONS

6. A house cost $145,987. Write this amount in word form.

_____

_____

7. Jorge has 100 dimes. How much money is that?

_____

EVERYDAY MATH CONNECTION

When you write a bank check, you fill in the amount both in standard form and in word form. Write the standard form or word form of the number where it is missing on the check.

8.

Jane Doe		2840
56 Fifth Street		
Math, FL 11111		

Pay to the Order of ___ Ace Roofing Co. ___ $ _____

One thousand, two hundred ninety and no cents _____ **Dollars**

First Bank _____ *Jane Doe* _____

9.

Jane Doe		2841
56 Fifth Street		
Math, FL 11111		

Pay to the Order of ___ Star Window Co. ___ $ *745.10*

_____ **Dollars**

First Bank _____ *Jane Doe* _____

Place Value to Hundred Millions

Write the value of each underlined digit in two ways.

1. 1<u>9</u>8,975,482 _____   _____

2. <u>9</u>00,087,360 _____   _____

Write two other forms of each number.

3. 100,070,000 _____   _____

4. 200,000,000 + 500,000 + 4,000 + 900 + 8

_____

_____

5. seventy million, eighty-four thousand, thirty-nine

_____

_____

MIXED APPLICATIONS

6. The *New York Times* had a daily circulation of about 1,149,000 during a recent six-month period. What number is one thousand more than 1,149,000? Write it in two different ways.

_____

_____

7. The *Chicago Tribune* had a daily circulation of about 740,000 during a recent six-month period. What number is one thousand less than 740,000? Write it in two different ways.

_____

_____

HISTORY CONNECTION

8. The first German newspaper was published in 1609. Write this number in word form.

_____

_____

9. The *New York Sun* was first published in 1830. Write this number in expanded form.

_____

_____

Model Place Value Relationships

Write the value of the underlined digit.

1. 6,0<u>3</u>5   2. 43,<u>7</u>82   3. 506,0<u>8</u>7   4. 4<u>9</u>,254

_____   _____   _____   _____

5. 1<u>3</u>6,422   6. 673,<u>5</u>12   7. <u>8</u>14,295   8. 736,1<u>4</u>4

_____   _____   _____   _____

Compare the values of the underlined digits.

9. 6,<u>3</u>00 and 5<u>3</u>0

The value of 3 in _____ is ____ times

the value of 3 in _____.

10. <u>2</u>,783 and 7,<u>2</u>83

The value of 2 in _____ is ____ times

the value of 2 in _____.

11. 3<u>4</u>,258 and <u>4</u>7,163

The value of 4 in _____ is ____ times

the value of 4 in _____.

12. 503,49<u>7</u> and 26,4<u>7</u>5

The value of 7 in _____ is ____ times

the value of 7 in _____.

SPORTS CONNECTION

Use the table for Exercises 13–14.

13. What is the value of the digit 9 in the attendance at the Redskins vs. Titans game?

_____

14. The attendance at which game has a 7 in the ten thousands place?

_____

FOOTBALL GAME ATTENDANCE	
Game	**Attendance**
Redskins vs. Titans	69,143
Ravens vs. Panthers	73,021
Patriots vs. Colts	68,756

Name _____ Date _____

Rename Numbers

Rename the number. Use the place-value chart to help.

1. 760 hundreds = _____

THOUSANDS			ONES		
Hundreds	Tens	Ones	Hundreds	Tens	Ones

2. 805 tens = _____

THOUSANDS			ONES		
Hundreds	Tens	Ones	Hundreds	Tens	Ones

3. 24 ten thousands = _____

THOUSANDS			ONES		
Hundreds	Tens	Ones	Hundreds	Tens	Ones

Rename the number.

4. 720 = _____ tens

5. 4 thousands 7 hundreds = _____

6. 25,600 = _____ hundreds

7. 204 thousands = _____

EVERYDAY MATH CONNECTION

8. For the fair, the organizers ordered 32 rolls of tickets. Each roll of tickets has 100 tickets. How many tickets were ordered in all?

_____

9. An apple orchard sells apples in bags of 10. The orchard sold a total of 2,430 apples one day. How many bags of apples was this?

_____

Comparing and Ordering to Ten Thousands

Compare the numbers. Write <, >, or = in the ◯.

1. 5,809 ◯ 4,908
2. 9,042 ◯ 8,998
3. 2,468 ◯ 1,137
4. 23,412 ◯ 19,246
5. 18,590 ◯ 18,650
6. 45,847 ◯ 45,847

Write the numbers in order from least to greatest.

7.	8.	9.	10.
2,345	32,076	70,291	99,909
22,486	32,570	68,921	99,900
12,123	23,676	69,129	99,099

_____ _____ _____ _____

_____ _____ _____ _____

MIXED APPLICATIONS

11. Map A shows an area of 12,000 square miles. Map B shows 11,979 square miles. Which map shows a greater area?

_____

12. The area of Montana is one hundred forty-seven thousand, forty-six square miles. Write the area in standard form.

_____

SOCIAL STUDIES CONNECTION

13. Use the table to order the areas of the Great Lakes from greatest to least.

_____

_____

_____

_____

_____

AREAS OF THE GREAT LAKES	
Name	**Area (in square miles)**
Huron	23,000
Superior	31,700
Erie	9,910
Michigan	22,300
Ontario	7,550

9

Comparing Using Symbols

Compare the numbers. Write <, >, or = in the ◯.

1. 2,541 ◯ 986
2. 274 ◯ 279
3. 8,642 ◯ 764
4. 2,329 ◯ 3,329
5. 62,911 ◯ 58,012
6. 8,116 ◯ 18,611

Compare the numbers using the symbol that means *is less than*.

7. 52; 56 _____
8. 76; 67 _____
9. 1,339; 1,239 _____

Compare the numbers using the symbol that means *is greater than*.

10. 84; 48 _____
11. 2,049; 2,094 _____
12. 26,784; 26,847 _____

MIXED APPLICATIONS

13. Sharon hiked 1,875 meters to a lookout on Mount Royal. The peak is 1,000 meters higher than the lookout. Write the height of the peak.

_____

14. Gina's hiking club climbed 1,024 meters today. On the day before, they climbed 100 meters less. Write the number of meters they climbed yesterday.

_____

GEOGRAPHY CONNECTION

Use the table to answer the questions.

15. Which mountain is highest?

_____

16. Which mountain is lowest?

_____

17. Which mountain is higher, Mount Shasta or Mount Rainier?

_____

HEIGHTS OF SOME U.S. MOUNTAINS	
Mountain	**Height (in meters)**
Mount Shasta	4,317
Mount Rushmore	1,745
Mount McKinley	6,194
Mount Hood	3,426
Mount Rainier	4,392
Mount Whitney	4,418

10

Name _____ Date _____

Comparing and Ordering to Millions

Compare the numbers. Write <, >, or = in the ◯.

1. 1,234 ◯ 1,253

2. 125,980 ◯ 124,489

3. 23,911 ◯ 23,918

4. 546 ◯ 546

Order from least to greatest.

5. 2,345; 2,435; 2,347 _____

6. 2,345,567; 2,345,657; 2,435,657 _____

MIXED APPLICATIONS

7. A census showed that Alabama had 4,447,100 people, Oklahoma had 3,450,654 people, and Kentucky had 4,041,769 people. Order these states from the least populated to the most populated.

_____

_____

8. The same census showed that Wyoming had a population of 493,782. Write this number in two different ways.

_____

_____

GEOGRAPHY CONNECTION

9. The state of Wyoming has an area of 97,818 square miles, and its population in 2000 was 493,782. At the same time, the District of Columbia's population was 572,059. Explain why you think the population of Wyoming was less than the population of the District of Columbia.

_____

_____

_____

Rounding

Rounded numbers tell "about how many." Remember, when a number is halfway between two numbers, always round the number up.

Round to the nearest ten.

1. 57 _____ 2. 82 _____ 3. 49 _____ 4. 35 _____

5. 63 _____ 6. 76 _____ 7. 51 _____ 8. 99 _____

Round to the nearest hundred.

9. 471 _____ 10. 739 _____ 11. 850 _____ 12. 399 _____

13. 782 _____ 14. 456 _____ 15. 327 _____ 16. 218 _____

Round to the nearest thousand.

17. 2,537 _____ 18. 5,499 _____

19. 6,205 _____ 20. 3,668 _____

21. 8,763 _____ 22. 6,819 _____

23. 44,174 _____ 24. 3,674 _____

NUMBER SENSE

25. There were 12,684 people at a concert. Which gives the closest estimate of the number of people at the concert—rounding to the nearest hundred or rounding to the nearest thousand? Explain.

_____

_____

_____

Rounding to Millions

Round to the nearest ten.

1. 34 _____ 2. 235 _____ 3. 450 _____

Round to the nearest hundred.

4. 875 _____ 5. 1,789 _____ 6. 45,824 _____

Round to the nearest thousand.

7. 3,457 _____ 8. 23,532 _____ 9. 124,890 _____

Round to the nearest ten thousand.

10. 45,999 _____ 11. 123,409 _____ 12. 578,123 _____

Round to the nearest hundred thousand.

13. 123,981 _____ 14. 1,461,234 _____ 15. 2,361,528 _____

Round to the nearest million.

16. 56,891,789 _____ 17. 156,148,901 _____

MIXED APPLICATIONS

Use the table for Exercises 18 and 19.

18. Round the depth of the Bering Sea to the nearest hundred feet.

    _____

19. Which ocean has a maximum depth of about 18,000 feet?

    _____

MAXIMUM DEPTHS	
Body of Water	**Depth (in feet)**
Atlantic Ocean	30,246
Arctic Ocean	17,881
Bering Sea	13,750
Indian Ocean	24,442

MIXED REVIEW

Round to the nearest ten and then to the nearest thousand.

20. 2,346 _____ 21. 125,675 _____ 22. 1,234,499 _____

  _____ _____ _____

13

Name _____ Date _____

Rounding Whole Numbers and Decimals

Estimate by rounding to the nearest ten or the nearest ten cents.

1. 52 _____
2. $3.78 _____
3. 66 _____
4. $2.45 _____

5. 87 _____
6. $1.34 _____
7. 555 _____
8. 226 _____

Estimate by rounding to the nearest hundred or to the nearest dollar.

9. 457 _____
10. 242 _____
11. $8.46 _____
12. 233 _____

Estimate by rounding to the nearest thousand.

13. 6,816 _____
14. 2,310 _____

15. 2,737 _____
16. 1,421 _____

MIXED APPLICATIONS

17. The world's longest river is the Nile. It is about 4,160 miles long. Estimate the length to the nearest hundred miles.

_____

18. The length of the Potomac River when rounded to the nearest ten miles is 380 miles. What is the least and the greatest length in miles that it could be?

_____

SOCIAL STUDIES CONNECTION

Each statement contains a measurement that is rounded to the nearest ten miles. Find each actual length in the box and write it after the statement. You will not use all the numbers.

19. More than 30 bridges cross the 500-mile-long Seine River in France. _____

20. The longest river in Europe is the Volga. It is about 2,190 miles long. _____

21. The Arkansas River created many canyons in the United States. It is about 1,460 miles long. _____

ACTUAL LENGTHS (in miles)
428
496
1,459
1,488
2,194
2,201

14

Name _____ Date _____

Exploring Prime and Composite Numbers

For each number in the "Number" column, arrange cubes (or counters) to make as many different rectangles as you can. As you work, complete the table.

	Number	Arrangement of Rectangles	Factors in Arrangements	Number of Different Factors
1.	11	____ row(s) of ____ ____ row(s) of ____	_____ _____	_____
2.	12			
3.	13			
4.	14			

Write *prime* or *composite* for each number.

5. 11 _____   6. 12 _____

7. 13 _____   8. 14 _____

VISUAL THINKING

Write *prime* or *composite* for each arrangement. Give the number of factors for each.

9. □ □   _____

10.    _____

15

Name _____ Date _____

Factors, Primes, and Composites

List all of the factors of each number.

1. 6 _____ 2. 35 _____

3. 19 _____ 4. 39 _____

5. 44 _____ 6. 64 _____

7. 56 _____ 8. 80 _____

Classify each number as *prime* or *composite*.

9. 18 _____ 10. 3 _____

11. 19 _____ 12. 102 _____

13. 41 _____ 14. 63 _____

15. 11 _____ 16. 51 _____

MIXED APPLICATIONS

17. Cheryl brought 30 fruit bars to a party. List all of the ways she can arrange them on platters in equal rows.

_____

_____

_____

18. Sonya is setting up tables for the 24 people at the party. The same number of people will sit at each table, and no one will sit alone. How many people could she sit at each table? List all possibilities.

_____

_____

WRITER'S CORNER

19. Write a problem similar to Exercise 17 or Exercise 18. Use the facts you know about divisibility.

_____

_____

_____

Adding 2-Digit Numbers

Find the sum. In Exercises 1–18, circle the columns in which you need to regroup.

1. 46
    + 13

2. 16
    + 65

3. 27
    + 38

4. 67
    + 29

5. 68
    + 82

6. 57
    + 89

7. 95
    + 33

8. 28
    + 26

9. 29
    + 49

10. 87
    + 87

11. 33
    + 27

12. 91
    + 84

13. 84
    + 56

14. 23
    + 31

15. 73
    + 25

16. 57
    + 72

17. 97
    + 49

18. 43
    + 14

19. 67 + 96 = _____
20. 43 + 92 = _____
21. 37 + 98 = _____
22. 75 + 58 = _____
23. 25 + 91 = _____
24. 79 + 46 = _____

MIXED APPLICATIONS

The table shows the time it took for each team to finish the races. Complete the table to show each team's total time.

	Team	Race 1	Race 2	Total
	Race Times (in seconds)			
25.	Blue	65	78	
26.	White	83	95	
27.	Red	64	82	
28.	Green	92	69	

29. Which team finished both races in the least time? _____

30. Which team took the most time to finish both races? _____

LOGICAL REASONING

31.   74
    + 6☐
    ―――――
    1☐1

32.   ☐7
    + 3☐
    ―――――
    126

33.   9 7
    + 5☐
    ―――――
    ☐☐1

Adding 3-Digit Numbers

Find the sum. Circle the columns in which you need to regroup.

1. 348 + 236	**2.** 374 + 561	**3.** 733 + 548	**4.** 971 + 309	**5.** 150 + 236
6. 895 + 364	**7.** 584 + 263	**8.** 475 + 650	**9.** 692 + 897	**10.** 234 + 723
11. 165 + 632	**12.** 242 + 639	**13.** 760 + 486	**14.** 365 + 678	**15.** 173 + 445
16. $256 + 217	**17.** $233 + 378	**18.** $254 + 130	**19.** $445 + 680	**20.** $245 + 932

MIXED APPLICATIONS

21. The Easton Art Club paid $784 for a painting and $341 for a piece of sculpture. How much did the club pay for the two works of art?

_____

22. An art show has 368 pieces of jewelry and 293 pieces of pottery. How many pieces of jewelry and pottery are in the show?

_____

MIXED REVIEW

Round each number to the nearest ten.

23. 62 _____   **24.** 76 _____   **25.** 84 _____   **26.** 35 _____

27. $125 _____   **28.** $57 _____   **29.** $154 _____   **30.** $21 _____

Round each number to the nearest hundred.

31. 568 _____   **32.** 373 _____   **33.** 633 _____   **34.** 921 _____

35. $475 _____   **36.** $625 _____   **37.** $839 _____   **38.** $758 _____

Adding 3 or More Addends

Find the sum.

1.	2.	3.	4.	5.
32	45	537	6,904	2,408
40	33	624	137	39
+ 17	+ 57	+ 769	+ 3,264	+ 359

6.	7.	8.	9.	10.
15	98	$568	$983	$98
26	346	327	3,764	346
48	297	141	839	297
+ 37	+ 16	+ 84	+ 172	+ 49

MIXED APPLICATIONS

11. It took Marc 25 minutes to wash his car, 18 minutes to vacuum it, and 90 minutes to wax it. How many minutes did he spend cleaning his car?

_____

12. Marc bought these accessories for his car: a GPS system for $72, a satellite radio for $89, and an in-dash DVD for $149. How much money did he spend?

_____

13. Use the table. How many cars were washed each month?

March _____

April _____

May _____

ACE CAR WAX BUSINESS		
Month	**Number of Cars**	
	Wash Only	Wash and Wax
March	3,657	1,582
April	2,819	2,476
May	6,538	4,728

LOGICAL REASONING

Use each of the digits 1, 2, 3, 4, 5, 9 once. Write a digit in each box to make —

14. the least possible sum.

☐ ☐ ☐
+ ☐ ☐ ☐

15. the greatest possible sum.

☐ ☐ ☐
+ ☐ ☐ ☐

19

Adding Whole Numbers

Estimate the sum. If the estimated sum is greater than 5,000, find the exact sum.

1. 435 + 241	**2.** 589 + 24	**3.** 4,789 + 1,234	**4.** 5,987 + 2,134
5. 25,901 + 12,000	**6.** 45,123 + 13,498	**7.** 456 987 + 902	**8.** 1,754 2,180 + 1,456

Complete the table.

Problem	Estimate	Sum
1,205 + 2,884 = ☐	**9.** _____	**10.** _____
794 + 1,340 = ☐	**11.** _____	**12.** _____
23,031 + 10,853 = ☐	**13.** _____	**14.** _____
7,660 + 2,400 = ☐	**15.** _____	**16.** _____

MIXED APPLICATIONS

17. Diego has these scores in the javelin throw: 135 feet, 106 feet, and 116 feet. What is his combined score for the three throws?

18. Jenna runs 1 mile every day as a part of her exercise program. One mile is equal to 1,760 yards, Write this number in expanded notation.

SCIENCE CONNECTION

19. A science student needs 325 milliliters of water for an experiment. Beaker A contains 176 milliliters of water. Beaker B contains 152 milliliters of water. Is this enough water for the experiment? Explain.

Subtracting 2-Digit Numbers

Find the difference. In Exercises 1–18, circle the problems in which you need to regroup.

1. 79 − 25	**2.** 95 − 58	**3.** 87 − 76	**4.** 73 − 56	**5.** 43 − 39	**6.** 98 − 67
7. 80 − 29	**8.** 76 − 27	**9.** 42 − 3	**10.** 25 − 15	**11.** 76 − 34	**12.** 61 − 26
13. 51 − 49	**14.** 59 − 35	**15.** 84 − 39	**16.** 65 − 46	**17.** 47 − 15	**18.** 80 − 60

19. $53 - 45 =$ _____ **20.** $81 - 63 =$ _____ **21.** $78 - 52 =$ _____

22. $92 - 84 =$ _____ **23.** $93 - 37 =$ _____ **24.** $67 - 42 =$ _____

25. $45 - 32 =$ _____ **26.** $68 - 49 =$ _____ **27.** $80 - 29 =$ _____

MIXED APPLICATIONS

28. Harrison's Hardware Store received a shipment of 85 garden hoses. The store sold 18 of the hoses. How many garden hoses did the store have left?

_____

29. Mr. Harrison had 54 snow shovels in his store. After a sale, 8 shovels were left. How many shovels did Mr. Harrison sell?

_____

NUMBER SENSE

Write the other number sentences that belong to the family of facts.

30. $9 + 8 = 17$
 $17 - 9 = 8$

31. $2 + 9 = 11$
 $11 - 2 = 9$

32. $11 - 8 = 3$
 $11 - 3 = 8$

33. $5 + 6 = 11$
 $6 + 5 = 11$

_____ _____ _____ _____

21

Name _____ Date _____

Subtracting 3-Digit Numbers

Find the difference.

1. 517
    − 292

2. 789
    − 294

3. 793
    − 189

4. 747
    − 628

5. 641
    − 250

6. $837
    − 157

7. $635
    − 227

8. $726
    − 158

9. $642
    − 88

10. $455
    − 396

11. 806 − 257 = _____

12. 912 − 88 = _____

13. $634 − $558 = _____

14. $953 − $659 = _____

MIXED APPLICATIONS

The table shows the type and the quantity of fish Emilio's Fish Market received on Saturday. Use the table to answer the questions.

15. How much more trout than sole did the market receive?

_____

16. How many kilograms of fish did Emilio receive on Saturday?

_____

SATURDAY'S SHIPMENT	
Type of Fish	**Quantity (in kilograms)**
Trout	334
Whitefish	187
Flounder	435
Salmon	282
Sole	195

VISUAL THINKING

17. Circle the model that shows how you would regroup to solve the number sentence.

    252 − 37 = ☐

a.

b.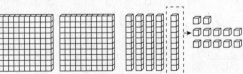

c.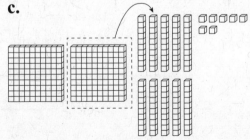

Subtracting Whole Numbers

Estimate each difference. If the estimated difference is greater than 20,000, find the exact difference.

1. $\begin{array}{r} 4,666 \\ -\ 1,888 \end{array}$	2. $\begin{array}{r} 44,874 \\ -\ 12,490 \end{array}$	3. $\begin{array}{r} 75,480 \\ -\ 54,371 \end{array}$	4. $\begin{array}{r} 34,159 \\ -\ 19,723 \end{array}$
5. $\begin{array}{r} 51,902 \\ -\ 20,921 \end{array}$	6. $\begin{array}{r} 11,774 \\ -\ 6,925 \end{array}$	7. $\begin{array}{r} 63,014 \\ -\ 2,364 \end{array}$	8. $\begin{array}{r} 34,567 \\ -\ 5,432 \end{array}$

MIXED APPLICATIONS

9. A football stadium can hold 88,550 fans. If 87,650 fans attend a football game, how many empty seats are there in the stadium?

_____

10. There were 24,789 fans at Monday's basketball game. There were 20,567 fans at Thursday's game. How many more fans attended the game on Monday than on Thursday?

_____

The all-time football rushing records were once held by Walter Payton (12,120 yd), Tony Dorsett (12,312 yd), Jim Brown (12,739 yd), and Franco Harris (16,726 yd).

11. Write these numbers in order from greatest to least.

_____

12. How many yards were rushed by Walter Payton and Tony Dorsett together?

_____

EVERYDAY MATH CONNECTION

**Companies use both calculators and computers to work with large numbers.
Use your calculator to solve.**

13. $10,232,000 - 9,342,000 = n$ _____

14. $9,932,200 + 82,400 = n$ _____

Subtracting Across Zeros

For each problem, show how you regrouped to find the difference.

1.   200
    − 123

2.   901
    − 279

3.   1,005
    − 509

4.   10,035
    − 9,172

Find the difference.

5.   607
    − 76

6.   400
    − 345

7.   209
    − 198

8.   6,000
    − 3,864

9.   5,900
    − 789

10.   4,002
    −   8

11.   10,087
    − 983

12.   30,030
    − 12,045

MIXED APPLICATIONS

13. Carlotta has 402 U.S. stamps and 87 Spanish stamps in her stamp collection. How many more U.S. stamps than Spanish stamps does she have in her collection?

14. Chen has 73 French stamps and 137 Greek stamps. Daniel has 123 French stamps and 42 Greek stamps. In total, Chen has how many more stamps than Daniel?

NUMBER SENSE

15. Show how you regroup. Solve.

    30,202
    − 24,311

16. For Exercise 15, explain why a 9 took the place of the 0 in thousands place but not the 0 in tens place.

_____

24

Addition and Subtraction

Use a calculator or pencil and paper to find each sum or difference.

1.   781
   + 397

2.   1,075
   − 397

3.   4,904
   + 2,097

4.   803
   − 157

5.   798
   + 4,806

6. 3,097 + 5,219 = _____

7. 6,004 − 1,997 = _____

MIXED APPLICATIONS

For Exercises 8–11, use the table.

AMIR'S NEWSSTAND					
Item	Newspaper	Magazine	Chapter Book	Puzzler Book	Comic Book
Cost	$2	$5	$9	$3	$4

8. How much change do you get from $20 if you buy a magazine and a comic book?

_____

9. How much change do you get from $15 if you buy a chapter book and a newspaper?

_____

10. How much will a magazine, a chapter book, and a puzzler book cost?

_____

11. Which two items together cost the same amount as a chapter book?

_____

CONSUMER CONNECTION

12. You have $12 to spend at the newsstand. Choose two items to buy and tell how much change you should receive.

Items	Cost	Change from $12

Add and Subtract with Greater Numbers

First, estimate the sum or difference. Then use a calculator or pencil and paper to find the exact answer.

1. 4,731 − 1,545	**2.** 5,789 + 1,861	**3.** 9,632 − 5,768	**4.** 3,569 + 4,483	**5.** 7,092 − 4,666
6. 2,739 + 1,985	**7.** 6,744 − 1,375	**8.** 5,837 − 2,678	**9.** 7,458 + 3,749	**10.** 6,832 + 2,818

11. $8,549 - 7,234 =$ _____   **12.** $4,960 - 3,879 =$ _____

13. $6,707 + 5,499 =$ _____   **14.** $43,476 - 30,908 =$ _____

MIXED APPLICATIONS

The table shows some readings on the electric meter at the Santa Fe Restaurant.

15. Complete the table. The "Amount Used" is the difference between the new reading and the last reading.

16. What was the total number of kilowatt hours used?

Meter Reading (in Kilowatt Hours)			
Month	**New Reading**	**Last Reading**	**Amount Used**
April	5,256	4,937	
May	8,107	5,256	
June	11,009	8,107	
July	12,142	11,009	

MIXED REVIEW

Compare. Write $<$, $>$, or $=$ in the $\bigcirc$.

17. 142 $\bigcirc$ 84

18. 52 $\bigcirc$ 252

19. 684 $\bigcirc$ 684

Find the sum or difference.

20. $14 + 76 + 30 + 41 =$ _____   **21.** $743 - 159 =$ _____

26

Connecting Addition and Subtraction

Find the sum or difference. Use the inverse operation to check your answer.

1.	832 + 254	_____ – _____	**2.**	638 – 199	_____ + _____	**3.**	7,323 + 2,107	_____ – _____

4.	8,145 + 7,008	_____ – _____	**5.**	14,098 – 10,123	_____ + _____	**6.**	25,187 – 8,865	_____ + _____

MIXED APPLICATIONS

7. Nick drove 139 miles on Saturday and 185 miles on Sunday. He says he drove 324 miles altogether. Is he correct? Explain.

_____

8. Sharla and Keisha took turns driving on their trip to California. Sharla drove 295 miles. Keisha drove 288 miles. About how long was their trip?

_____

MIXED REVIEW

Use mental math and properties of addition to find the missing number.

9. $8 + \square = 9 + 8$

10. $8 + 0 = \square$

11. $6 + (2 + \square) = (6 + 2) + 7$

Round to the nearest hundred. Then estimate the sum or difference.

12.	4,320 + 3,213	**13.**	3,091 – 1,342	**14.**	9,108 + 2,547	**15.**	7,187 – 5,526	**16.**	9,115 – 3,457

Use Exercises 12–16. Round to the nearest thousand.
Then estimate each sum or difference.

17. _____ **18.** _____ **19.** _____ **20.** _____ **21.** _____

2 and 3 as Factors

Draw an array to solve.

1. $2 \times 6 =$ _____   **2.** $3 \times 8 =$ _____   **3.** $2 \times 7 =$ _____

Find the product.

4. $\begin{array}{r} 2 \\ \times\, 1 \\ \hline \end{array}$ **5.** $\begin{array}{r} 2 \\ \times\, 4 \\ \hline \end{array}$ **6.** $\begin{array}{r} 3 \\ \times\, 1 \\ \hline \end{array}$ **7.** $\begin{array}{r} 2 \\ \times\, 8 \\ \hline \end{array}$ **8.** $\begin{array}{r} 3 \\ \times\, 6 \\ \hline \end{array}$ **9.** $\begin{array}{r} 3 \\ \times\, 8 \\ \hline \end{array}$

10. $\begin{array}{r} 2 \\ \times\, 9 \\ \hline \end{array}$ **11.** $\begin{array}{r} 2 \\ \times\, 5 \\ \hline \end{array}$ **12.** $\begin{array}{r} 2 \\ \times\, 6 \\ \hline \end{array}$ **13.** $\begin{array}{r} 3 \\ \times\, 9 \\ \hline \end{array}$ **14.** $\begin{array}{r} 2 \\ \times\, 7 \\ \hline \end{array}$ **15.** $\begin{array}{r} 2 \\ \times\, 2 \\ \hline \end{array}$

16. $\begin{array}{r} 3 \\ \times\, 4 \\ \hline \end{array}$ **17.** $\begin{array}{r} 2 \\ \times\, 3 \\ \hline \end{array}$ **18.** $\begin{array}{r} 3 \\ \times\, 5 \\ \hline \end{array}$ **19.** $\begin{array}{r} 3 \\ \times\, 2 \\ \hline \end{array}$ **20.** $\begin{array}{r} 3 \\ \times\, 7 \\ \hline \end{array}$ **21.** $\begin{array}{r} 3 \\ \times\, 3 \\ \hline \end{array}$

22. $8 \times 3 =$ _____   **23.** $5 \times 3 =$ _____   **24.** $6 \times 2 =$ _____   **25.** $9 \times 2 =$ _____

26. $4 \times 2 =$ _____   **27.** $7 \times 3 =$ _____   **28.** $1 \times 3 =$ _____   **29.** $8 \times 2 =$ _____

MIXED APPLICATIONS

30. Mike buys 5 packages of stamps. Each package contains 2 stamps. How many stamps does Mike buy?

_____

31. Mike buys packing tape for $4, a large mailing carton for $6, and a package of mailing labels for $5. How much does he spend?

_____

SPORTS CONNECTION

A touchdown in football is worth 6 points. A field goal is worth 3 points. How many points are scored for

32. 2 touchdowns and 5 field goals? _____

33. 3 touchdowns and 3 field goals? _____

34. 4 touchdowns and 2 field goals? _____

4 and 5 as Factors

Draw an array for each multiplication sentence.

1. $4 \times 5 = 20$ **2.** $5 \times 9 = 45$ **3.** $5 \times 8 = 40$

Find the product.

4. $\begin{array}{r} 5 \\ \times 3 \\ \hline \end{array}$
5. $\begin{array}{r} 5 \\ \times 5 \\ \hline \end{array}$
6. $\begin{array}{r} 4 \\ \times 1 \\ \hline \end{array}$
7. $\begin{array}{r} 5 \\ \times 2 \\ \hline \end{array}$
8. $\begin{array}{r} 4 \\ \times 6 \\ \hline \end{array}$
9. $\begin{array}{r} 5 \\ \times 6 \\ \hline \end{array}$

10. $\begin{array}{r} 4 \\ \times 3 \\ \hline \end{array}$
11. $\begin{array}{r} 5 \\ \times 7 \\ \hline \end{array}$
12. $\begin{array}{r} 4 \\ \times 8 \\ \hline \end{array}$
13. $\begin{array}{r} 4 \\ \times 4 \\ \hline \end{array}$
14. $\begin{array}{r} 5 \\ \times 3 \\ \hline \end{array}$
15. $\begin{array}{r} 5 \\ \times 4 \\ \hline \end{array}$

16. $\begin{array}{r} 5 \\ \times 9 \\ \hline \end{array}$
17. $\begin{array}{r} 4 \\ \times 2 \\ \hline \end{array}$
18. $\begin{array}{r} 5 \\ \times 1 \\ \hline \end{array}$
19. $\begin{array}{r} 4 \\ \times 5 \\ \hline \end{array}$
20. $\begin{array}{r} 5 \\ \times 8 \\ \hline \end{array}$
21. $\begin{array}{r} 4 \\ \times 9 \\ \hline \end{array}$

22. $5 \times 8 =$ _____ **23.** $5 \times 3 =$ _____ **24.** $5 \times 7 =$ _____ **25.** $9 \times 5 =$ _____

26. $5 \times 4 =$ _____ **27.** $4 \times 7 =$ _____ **28.** $4 \times 4 =$ _____ **29.** $8 \times 4 =$ _____

MIXED APPLICATIONS

30. There are 6 helicopters at the airport. Each helicopter can hold 5 people. How many people can all of the helicopters hold?

_____

31. Company A owns 5 helicopters. It buys 7 new helicopters. How many helicopters does Company A have now?

_____

NUMBER SENSE

Compare. Write $<$, $>$, or $=$ in the $\bigcirc$.

32. $4 \times 2 \bigcirc 9$ **33.** $7 \times 3 \bigcirc 20$ **34.** $6 \times 2 \bigcirc 12$

35. $25 \bigcirc 8 \times 3$ **36.** $6 \times 3 \bigcirc 9 \times 2$ **37.** $5 \times 3 \bigcirc 8 \times 2$

6 and 7 as Factors

Draw an array for each multiplication sentence. Find the product.

1. $6 \times 7 =$ _____

2. $7 \times 4 =$ _____

3. $6 \times 9 =$ _____

Find the product.

4.	7 $\times 6$	5.	6 $\times 1$	6.	7 $\times 1$	7.	6 $\times 7$	8.	7 $\times 2$

9.	7 $\times 4$	10.	6 $\times 3$	11.	7 $\times 7$	12.	6 $\times 6$

13. $6 \times 8 =$ _____

14. $8 \times 7 =$ _____

15. $9 \times 8 =$ _____

16. $2 \times 7 =$ _____

17. $6 \times 6 =$ _____

18. $7 \times 3 =$ _____

19. $6 \times 9 =$ _____

20. $5 \times 6 =$ _____

MIXED APPLICATIONS

21. Employees at the music store put new strings on 7 violins. Each violin gets 4 strings. How many strings are used?

_____

22. The Wilson School has 7 pianos. If 2 of the pianos need repair, how many pianos are in working order?

_____

LOGICAL REASONING

23. The multiplication wheel has a factor at the center, factors in the middle circle, and products in the outer circle. Find each missing product or factor.

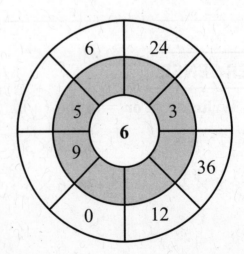

8 and 9 as Factors

Draw an array to solve. Find the product.

1. $4 \times 8 =$ _____   2. $3 \times 9 =$ _____   3. $8 \times 8 =$ _____

Find the product.

4.	9	5.	8	6.	9	7.	8	8.	9	9.	8
	$\times 8$		$\times 3$		$\times 1$		$\times 7$		$\times 2$		$\times 1$

10.	9	11.	8	12.	8	13.	8	14.	9	15.	8
	$\times 7$		$\times 4$		$\times 9$		$\times 8$		$\times 6$		$\times 2$

16.	9	17.	8	18.	9	19.	9	20.	9	21.	8
	$\times 5$		$\times 6$		$\times 9$		$\times 3$		$\times 4$		$\times 5$

MIXED APPLICATIONS

22. A baker can make 8 batches of muffins each hour. How many batches can the baker make in 7 hours?

_____

23. The baker has 8 rows of muffins on a baking sheet. There are 6 muffins in each row. How many muffins are there?

_____

VISUAL THINKING

24. Circle the letter of the correct number sentence to help you find the number of cookies on the baking sheet. Then solve.

   a. $4 \times 4 = ?$

   b. $(4 \times 4) - 2 = ?$

   c. $(4 \times 4) + 2 = ?$

   _____ cookies

31

Mental Math

PRACTICING MULTIPLICATION FACTS

Find the product.

1. $\begin{array}{r} 8 \\ \times\,3 \\ \hline \end{array}$	**2.** $\begin{array}{r} 9 \\ \times\,6 \\ \hline \end{array}$	**3.** $\begin{array}{r} 8 \\ \times\,4 \\ \hline \end{array}$	**4.** $\begin{array}{r} 3 \\ \times\,6 \\ \hline \end{array}$	**5.** $\begin{array}{r} 7 \\ \times\,8 \\ \hline \end{array}$	**6.** $\begin{array}{r} 5 \\ \times\,4 \\ \hline \end{array}$
7. $\begin{array}{r} 6 \\ \times\,0 \\ \hline \end{array}$	**8.** $\begin{array}{r} 4 \\ \times\,4 \\ \hline \end{array}$	**9.** $\begin{array}{r} 8 \\ \times\,9 \\ \hline \end{array}$	**10.** $\begin{array}{r} 4 \\ \times\,6 \\ \hline \end{array}$	**11.** $\begin{array}{r} 7 \\ \times\,5 \\ \hline \end{array}$	**12.** $\begin{array}{r} 9 \\ \times\,9 \\ \hline \end{array}$
13. $\begin{array}{r} 4 \\ \times\,7 \\ \hline \end{array}$	**14.** $\begin{array}{r} 5 \\ \times\,6 \\ \hline \end{array}$	**15.** $\begin{array}{r} 9 \\ \times\,7 \\ \hline \end{array}$	**16.** $\begin{array}{r} 4 \\ \times\,4 \\ \hline \end{array}$	**17.** $\begin{array}{r} 0 \\ \times\,8 \\ \hline \end{array}$	**18.** $\begin{array}{r} 7 \\ \times\,6 \\ \hline \end{array}$

Find the product.

19. $8 \times 8 =$ _____ **20.** $7 \times 3 =$ _____ **21.** $8 \times 6 =$ _____ **22.** $7 \times 7 =$ _____

23. $6 \times 1 =$ _____ **24.** $4 \times 9 =$ _____ **25.** $9 \times 0 =$ _____ **26.** $5 \times 9 =$ _____

Complete each multiplication table.

27.

$\times$	0	1	2	3	4	5	6	7	8	9
8	0	8	16							

28.

$\times$	0	1	2	3	4	5	6	7	8	9
7	0	7	14							

MIXED APPLICATIONS

29. There are 6 ears of yellow corn and 2 ears of white corn in each bag. There are 8 bags. How many ears of corn are there?

30. A grocer puts 3 green peppers in each of 8 packages. He puts 5 green peppers in the ninth package. How many green peppers is this?

MIXED REVIEW

Find the sum or difference.

31. $\begin{array}{r} 6{,}375 \\ +\ \ 739 \\ \hline \end{array}$	**32.** $\begin{array}{r} 5{,}485 \\ -\,2{,}676 \\ \hline \end{array}$	**33.** $\begin{array}{r} 1{,}805 \\ +\,2{,}676 \\ \hline \end{array}$	**34.** $\begin{array}{r} 8{,}872 \\ -\,2{,}963 \\ \hline \end{array}$	**35.** $\begin{array}{r} 2{,}544 \\ -\ \ 878 \\ \hline \end{array}$

Multiplication Comparisons

Write a comparison sentence.

1. $6 \times 3 = 18$

_____ times as many as _____ is _____ .

2. $63 = 7 \times 9$

_____ is _____ times as many as _____ .

3. $5 \times 4 = 20$

_____ times as many as _____ is _____ .

4. $48 = 8 \times 6$

_____ is _____ times as many as _____ .

Write an equation.

5. 2 times as many as 8 is 16.

_____

6. 42 is 6 times as many as 7.

_____

7. 3 times as many as 5 is 15.

_____

8. 36 is 9 times as many as 4.

_____

9. 72 is 8 times as many as 9.

_____

10. 5 times as many as 6 is 30.

_____

MIXED APPLICATIONS

11. Alan is 14 years old. This is twice as old as his brother James is. How old is James?

_____

12. There are 27 campers. This is nine times as many as the number of counselors. How many counselors are there?

_____

33

Comparison Problems

Draw a model. Write an equation and solve.

1. Stacey made a necklace using 4 times as many blue beads as red beads. She used a total of 40 beads. How many blue beads did Stacey use? (Think: Stacey used a total of 40 beads. Let n represent the number of red beads and $4n$ represent the number of blue beads.)

   _$n + 4n = 40$, so $5n = 40$_
   _____

2. At the zoo, there were 3 times as many monkeys as lions. Tom counted a total of 24 monkeys and lions. How many monkeys were there? (Think: There are 24 animals. Let n represent the number of lions and $3n$ represent the number of monkeys.)

   _____

   _____

3. Fred's frog jumped 7 times as far as Al's frog. The two frogs jumped a total of 56 inches. How far did Fred's frog jump?

   _____

4. Sheila has 5 times as many markers as Dave. Together, they have 18 markers. How many markers does Sheila have?

   _____

LOGICAL REASONING

5. Rafael counted a total of 40 white cars and yellow cars. There were 9 times as many white cars as yellow cars. How many white cars did Rafael count?

   _____

6. Sue scored a total of 35 points in two games. She scored 6 times as many points in the second game as in the first. How many more points did she score in the second game?

   _____

Name _____ Date _____

Dividing by 2 and 3

Draw a picture to solve.

1. $9 \div 3 =$ _____

2. $12 \div 2 =$ _____

3. $18 \div 2 =$ _____

Find the quotient.

4. $27 \div 3 =$ _____ **5.** $3 \div 3 =$ _____ **6.** $18 \div 3 =$ _____ **7.** $4 \div 2 =$ _____

8. $8 \div 2 =$ _____ **9.** $21 \div 3 =$ _____ **10.** $14 \div 2 =$ _____ **11.** $15 \div 3 =$ _____

12. $2\overline{)16}$ **13.** $3\overline{)6}$ **14.** $3\overline{)27}$ **15.** $3\overline{)24}$

16. $2\overline{)4}$ **17.** $3\overline{)15}$ **18.** $3\overline{)24}$ **19.** $2\overline{)6}$

20. $2\overline{)10}$ **21.** $3\overline{)18}$ **22.** $3\overline{)12}$ **23.** $2\overline{)2}$

MIXED APPLICATIONS

24. There are 16 puppies at doggie play day. At naptime, they are placed two to a cage. How many cages are used?

_____

25. There are 24 bags of dog food in the storage room. If 3 bags are used each day, for how many days will the dog food last?

_____

VISUAL THINKING

Draw a picture of each quotient.

26.

27.

28.

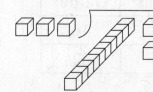 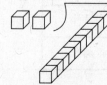 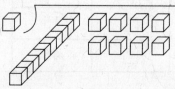 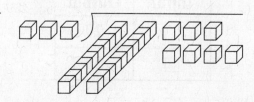

35

Unit 3
Core Skills Math, Grade 4

Name _____   Date _____

Dividing by 4 and 5

Draw a picture to solve.

1. $30 \div 5 =$ _____

2. $20 \div 4 =$ _____

3. $25 \div 5 =$ _____

Find the quotient.

4. $40 \div 5 =$ _____ **5.** $28 \div 4 =$ _____ **6.** $15 \div 5 =$ _____ **7.** $32 \div 4 =$ _____

8. $35 \div 5 =$ _____ **9.** $16 \div 4 =$ _____ **10.** $36 \div 4 =$ _____ **11.** $5 \div 5 =$ _____

12. $4\overline{)20}$

13. $5\overline{)25}$

14. $4\overline{)12}$

15. $5\overline{)30}$

16. $5\overline{)45}$

17. $4\overline{)8}$

MIXED APPLICATIONS

18. Mrs. Thomas has 45 reading books in her classroom. Each shelf will hold 9 books. How many bookshelves are needed to hold the 45 books?

_____

19. Mr. Dalton spent $45 on a new calculator for the math club. He gave the salesclerk $60. How much change should he get?

_____

LOGICAL REASONING

Find the missing factors to complete each table.

20.

Multiply by 4	
Input	Output
□	20
□	36

21.

Multiply by 5	
Input	Output
□	15
□	45

22.

Multiply by □	
Input	Output
2	16
4	32

36

Dividing by 6 and 7

Draw a picture to solve.

1. 35 ÷ 7 = _____   **2.** 36 ÷ 6 = _____   **3.** 21 ÷ 7 = _____

Find the quotient.

4. 14 ÷ 7 = _____ **5.** 42 ÷ 6 = _____ **6.** 18 ÷ 6 = _____ **7.** 63 ÷ 7 = _____

8. 30 ÷ 6 = _____ **9.** 54 ÷ 6 = _____ **10.** 7 ÷ 7 = _____ **11.** 42 ÷ 7 = _____

12. 6)‾24‾   **13.** 7)‾28‾   **14.** 6)‾12‾

15. 7)‾49‾   **16.** 6)‾6‾   **17.** 7)‾56‾

MIXED APPLICATIONS

18. Jason earns $63 each day as a ticket agent. He usually works 7 hours per day. Last Sunday he worked only 5 hours. How much money did he earn last Sunday?

_____

19. The express train runs for 6 hours each day and makes 24 trips. It makes the same number of trips each hour. How many trips does the train make each hour?

_____

LOGICAL REASONING

Write whether you will divide to find *how many groups* or to find *how many in each group*. Solve.

20. The gas station puts 24 new tires on 6 cars. Each car gets the same number of tires. How many tires does each car get?

_____

21. Mr. Feldman has 40 new car mirrors. There are 5 mirrors in each box. How many boxes of mirrors are there?

_____

37

Name _____   Date _____

Dividing by 8 and 9

Draw a picture to solve.

1. 36 ÷ 9 = _____   **2.** 40 ÷ 8 = _____   **3.** 27 ÷ 9 = _____

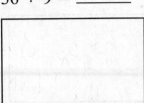 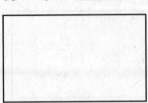 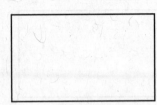

Find the quotient.

4. 56 ÷ 8 = _____   **5.** 18 ÷ 9 = _____   **6.** 24 ÷ 8 = _____   **7.** 63 ÷ 9 = _____

8. 32 ÷ 8 = _____   **9.** 8 ÷ 8 = _____   **10.** 45 ÷ 9 = _____   **11.** 72 ÷ 8 = _____

12. 9)54   **13.** 8)64   **14.** 8)48   **15.** 9)72

16. 9)9   **17.** 8)16   **18.** 9)81   **19.** 9)27

20. 8)24   **21.** 8)56   **22.** 9)18   **23.** 8)32

MIXED APPLICATIONS

24. A florist used 56 roses to make 8 bouquets. The same number of roses is in each bouquet. How many roses are in each bouquet?

_____

25. Ms. Cohen makes 6 baskets of flowers for a party. She uses 9 flowers in each basket. How many flowers does she use?

_____

MIXED REVIEW

Write three other facts for each fact family.

26. 9 × 5 = 45   **27.** 48 ÷ 6 = 8   **28.** 8 × 9 = 72

_____   _____   _____

_____   _____   _____

_____   _____   _____

38

Problem Solving

CHOOSE A STRATEGY

> **STRATEGIES**
> • Make a Table to Analyze Data
> • Find a Pattern
> • Draw a Picture

Choose a strategy and solve.

1. A farmer has 72 chickens. There are 9 chickens in each pen. How many pens of chickens does the farmer have?

_____

2. The farmer uses 2 bags of feed each day. How many bags of feed does the farmer use in one week?

_____

3. Henry spends 280 minutes a week training his new puppy. He works with his puppy twice a day, in the morning and in the afternoon. Each training session is the same length. What is the length of each training session in minutes?

_____

4. Della exercised her pony for 15 minutes on the first day, 20 minutes on the second day, 25 minutes on the third day, and so on. At this rate of increase, how many minutes of exercise will the pony get on the seventh day?

_____

VISUAL THINKING

Write a multiplication number sentence to tell how many.

5. How many ? _____

6. How many ? _____

7. How many ? _____

8. How many  ? _____

39

Name _____ Date _____

Time: Estimation

Choose the most reasonable estimation of time for each. Write *seconds*, *minutes*, *hours*, *days*, *weeks*, *months*, or *years*.

1. Summer lasts about 3 __months__ .

2. To eat your lunch takes about 20 __min__ .

3. It takes about 10 __min__ to take a shower.

4. It takes about one ~~min~~ second to snap your fingers.

Choose the best estimate for each.

5. The time it takes to eat dinner

   a. 30 minutes
   b. 30 hours
   c. 30 days

6. The amount of time in a good night's sleep

   a. 8 seconds
   b. 8 minutes
   c. 8 hours

MIXED APPLICATIONS

7. Jeff's piano lesson usually lasts for about an hour. Today, his lesson started at 2:55 P.M. At about what time will today's lesson be over?

   _3:55_

8. Alice practiced playing the violin for 15 minutes. Then she practiced the piano for 35 minutes. Was her total practice time more or less than 1 hour?

   50. min
   less than hour

LOGICAL REASONING

9. Draw the hands on the last two clocks to complete the pattern.

Unit 4
Core Skills Math, Grade 4

Exploring Elapsed Time

Tell how much time has elapsed.

1.

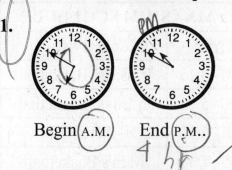

Begin A.M.   End P.M..

_____ 4 hr _____

2.

Begin A.M.   End P.M.

_____ 1 hr 5 min _____

Use the clocks to help you answer Exercises 3–5.

3. How many minutes pass from 1:20 P.M. to 1:55 P.M.?

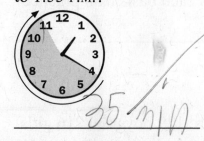

_____ 35 min _____

4. How many hours pass from 9:00 A.M. to 2:00 P.M.?

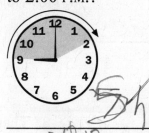

_____ 5 hr _____

5. What is the time when it is 30 minutes before 8:15 A.M.?

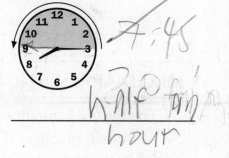

7:45

half an hour

_____

MIXED APPLICATIONS

6. Luis went outside to ride his bike at 3:35 P.M. His mother told him to be home by 4:10 P.M. How long did Luis have to ride his bike?

_____ 35 min _____

7. Mr. Baxter wants to leave his house at 8:00 in the morning. He needs 50 minutes to get ready. What time should he get up?

_____ 7:10 _____

SCIENCE CONNECTION

8. Brenda works at a hospital. She takes blood samples from patients every 45 minutes. She takes the first sample at 10:15 A.M. and the last sample at 1:15 P.M. Write the times when Brenda took a sample.

First Sample ____10:15____   Second Sample ____1:00____

Third Sample____11:45____   Fourth Sample ____12:30____

Last Sample ____1:15____

Using a Schedule

Use the gymnasium schedule for Exercises 1–6.

GYMNASIUM SCHEDULE	
Time	**Activity**
3:30–4:15	Jr. Girls' Basketball
4:30–5:15	Jr. Boys' Basketball
5:30–6:30	Aerobics
6:45–7:30	Men's Basketball

1. Sean is a 9-year-old boy. At what time does his basketball practice begin?

   4:30

2. Tom is a 35-year-old man. At what time does his basketball practice begin?

   6:45

3. Which activity is taking place at 7:00?

   Men's Basketball

4. At what time is Luisa's aerobics class over?

   6:30

5. How long is the aerobics class?

   1 hr

6. How long is each basketball practice?

   45 min   45 min   and   1 hr   25 min

MIXED APPLICATIONS

7. Thad was 15 minutes late to basketball practice. If it began at 6:35, at what time did Thad arrive?

   6:50

8. There are 129 boys and 216 girls watching the basketball game. How many boys and girls are watching?

   216   345
   + 129
   345

EVERYDAY MATH CONNECTION

9. Write your school schedule for today. Tell the time you will have reading and math. Tell the time you will have lunch and recess.

Time	Activity
_____	_____
_____	_____
_____	_____
_____	_____
_____	_____

Problem Solving

USE A TABLE OR A SCHEDULE

Use the train schedule to answer Exercises 1–4.

1. Which train arrives in Linden at 10:05 A.M.?

   _B_

2. Which train arrives in Layton before 9:00 A.M.?

   _A_

3. How many trains stop in the morning at Fairfax?

   _2_

4. How long does it take Train A to go from Edison to Sunset?

   15 min

Weekday Train Schedule – Arrivals			
Station	**Train A**	**Train B**	**Train C**
	A.M.	A.M.	P.M.
Edison	7:12	9:00	12:10
Sunset	7:27	9:15	12:25
Fairfax	7:52	——	12:50
Woodruff	——	9:47	1:02
Linden	8:18	10:05	1:20
Layton	8:51	10:38	1:53

MIXED APPLICATIONS

STRATEGIES
• Find a Pattern • Draw a Picture • Write a Number Sentence

5. Train D stops every 20 minutes. The first stop is Landville at 9:00 A.M. What time is it when Train D makes its seventh stop in Delray?

   _11 AM_

6. A ticket for a trip from Wayne to Centerville costs $26. A trip from Ardmore to Beltsville costs $19. Find the difference between the costs of the two tickets.

   _7_

SPORTS CONNECTION

Recorded times for many athletic events include seconds. Tell how long each of the following events took.

2 hours → 2 : 16 : 37 ← 37 seconds

16 minutes

7. 3 : 36 : 14 ____ three hr, thirty six min, and

8. 6 : 42 : 05 ____

Problem-Solving Strategy

WORK BACKWARD

Solve. Use a clock face.

1. Pablo got to the meeting 1 hour late. The time was 10:15. When did the meeting begin?

   9:15

2. Martin spent 2 hours and 15 minutes in the library. He left the library at 4:30. What time did he arrive?

   2:15

3. Jeff returned from his errands at 2:00. He had been gone for 2 hours and 30 minutes. At what time did he leave?

   12:30

4. Rosa thought of a number and added 5. She subtracted 3 and doubled the difference. What number did she begin with if her final number is 10?

   7

MIXED APPLICATIONS

STRATEGIES
• Act It Out • Work Backward
• Guess and Check • Draw a Picture

Choose a strategy and solve.

5. Sue must be home from the mall by 3:30. It takes 45 minutes to get home. What time must Sue leave the mall?

   4:15

6. Debra poses for a photo with her three brothers. Debra is next to Matt. Len is between Debra and Andy. Andy is on the left end. Order them from left to right.

   A L D M

   ALDM

EVERYDAY MATH CONNECTION

Write *hours* or *minutes* to complete each sentence.

7. Lauren does homework for 30 _____ min _____ each night.

8. Mick is at school for 6 _____ hr _____ each weekday.

9. Cassie has art class for 45 _____ min _____ each week.

10. Yoshi runs 1 mile in 10 _____ min _____ .

Name _____ Date _____

Units of Time

Complete. Use a calculator to help you. Use 1 year = 365 days.

1. 4 years = _____ months

2. 19 minutes = _____ seconds

3. 3 weeks = _____ days

4. 7 days = _____ hours

5. 2 years = _____ days

6. 72 hours = _____ days

7. 108 months = _____ years

8. 6 hours = _____ minutes = _____ seconds

9. 91 days = _____ weeks

10. 192 hours = _____ days = _____ minutes

11. 2 years = _____ hours

12. 3 hours 22 minutes = _____ minutes

13. 1 week = _____ seconds

14. 210 hours = _____ days _____ hours

15. 208 weeks = _____ years

16. 62 months = _____ years _____ months

MIXED APPLICATIONS

17. How many minutes are there in 2 weeks?

_____

18. How many days are there in four consecutive years? (Hint: leap year = 366 days)

_____

19. Anita volunteers at a local school for 3 hours each day. How many hours does she volunteer in a 180-day school year?

_____

20. Dennis' father wants him to study 5 hours every week. So far this week he has studied 45 minutes for each of the last 4 nights. How much more time must he study this week?

_____

EVERYDAY MATH CONNECTION

21. Explain the steps you would take to change the unit of time from days to weeks. Then explain the steps you would take to change from years to minutes.

_____

_____

_____

Comparing Amounts of Money

Circle the letter that shows the same amount of money.

1.    a.    b.    c.

2.    a.    b.    c.

MIXED APPLICATIONS

3. A package of hair clips costs $6.49. Gilda has one $5 bill, one $1 bill, and 4 nickels. How much more money does she need?

4. Hans earns $5.00 babysitting. He wants to buy a board game for $3.95 and a comic book for $0.75. Does he have enough money?

5. Lani has one $5 bill, two $1 bills, 3 quarters, 3 dimes, and 4 pennies. Can she buy a book for $6.95?

6. Wes wants to buy a kite for $5.49, string for $2.25, and ribbon for $1.79. How much do the three items cost?

MIXED REVIEW

Find the sum or difference.

7.	8.	9.	10.	11.
$5.95	$2.97	$8.00	$9.70	$6.59
+ 1.79	+ 8.25	− 2.49	+ 2.43	− 4.95

Unit 4
Core Skills Math, Grade 4

Name _____ Date _____

Problem Solving

IDENTIFY REASONABLE RESULTS

A snack bar shows these prices.

Bagel, plain	$1.49	Tuna Sandwich	$3.75
Bagel, with cream cheese	$2.25	Turkey Sandwich	$4.25
Potato Salad (1 pt)	$2.75	Fish Taco	$5.99
Coleslaw (1 pt)	$2.25	Veggie Burger	$4.49
Pickles (2)	$1	Soup, small/large	$2.99/$3.99

Use mental math to find if the total cost is reasonable. Then circle *Yes* or *No*.

1. Renée buys a plain bagel, coleslaw, and a small soup.

   Cost: about $12

   Yes   No

2. Pablo buys a tuna sandwich and a pint of potato salad.

   Cost: about $7

   Yes   No

3. Adrienne buys 2 fish tacos and 2 large soups.

   Cost: about $10

   Yes   No

4. Kevin buys a veggie burger, pickles, and some coleslaw.

   Cost: about $8

   Yes   No

Use mental math and/or estimation to decide if the amount of change is reasonable. Then circle *Yes* or *No*.

5. Yuki buys some potato salad, a small soup, and a turkey sandwich. She pays with a $20 bill.   Change: $5.25   Yes   No

6. Reggie buys a veggie burger, a bagel with cream cheese, and a large soup. He pays with a $10 and $5 bill.   Change: $4.27   Yes   No

7. Jennifer buys a turkey sandwich and a small soup. She pays with a $10 bill.   Change: $2.75   Yes   No

MIXED APPLICATIONS

8. Bella makes necklaces using 10 blue beads and 5 gold beads. She says that she uses 60 beads to make 4 necklaces. Is this reasonable? Explain.

   _____

   _____

9. Chen rides his bike 3.5 miles every day. He estimates that over 180 days he rides more than 1,000 miles. Is his estimate reasonable? Explain.

   _____

Problem-Solving Strategy

ACT IT OUT

Solve. Use money manipulatives if they are helpful.

1. Uma bought a pen for $1.29. She paid for it with 9 coins. What coins did she use?

   _____

   _____

2. Lucia bought a notebook for $5.95. List two combinations of bills and coins she could use to pay for the notebook.

   _____

   _____

MIXED APPLICATIONS

> **STRATEGIES**
> • Guess and Check • Work Backward
> • Act It Out • Draw a Picture
> • Write a Number Sentence

Choose a strategy and solve.

3. Mel has saved $9.42. He earns $4.50 mowing the lawn. How much money does he have now?

   _____

4. Don paid for a pen with a $10 bill. His change is $6.84. What was the cost of the pen?

   _____

5. On Monday Lani added 7 dimes to her bank. Then she spent 5 dimes. Now she has 12 dimes. How many dimes did she have to begin with?

   _____

6. Carol bought a puzzle book for $1.80. She gave the clerk 9 coins to pay for it. What coins did Carol use to pay for the puzzle book?

   _____

EVERYDAY MATH CONNECTION

7. Write the amounts that show how to count 5 coins as the change for a $1.34 purchase paid for with two $1 bills.

   _____

48

Problem Solving

MAKE CHOICES

CRAFT PLUS PRICES					
Markers		**Paints**		**Clothes**	
Thin	$0.69	Puffy	$1.00	Vest	$13.98
Medium	1.05	Glitter	1.95	Jacket	18.00
Wide	1.90	Neon	2.50	Sweatshirt	8.75

1. Wayne buys a vest. He has $3 left to spend at Craft Plus. He wants to buy paint and a marker. What choices of paint and marker can he make?

_____

_____

2. Edie has $20 to spend on clothes, paint, and a marker at Craft Plus. What choices can she make if she buys one of each type of item?

_____

_____

MIXED APPLICATIONS

> **STRATEGIES**
> • Act It Out • Guess and Check
> • Make a Model • Write a Number Sentence

Choose a strategy and solve.

3. Use the prices above. Tilo buys a vest, a thin marker, and neon paint. What is the total cost?

_____

4. Sofia buys 7 markers and 3 times as many paints. How many paints does she buy?

_____

WRITER'S CORNER

5. Imagine that you can buy and decorate an item of clothing at Crafts Plus. Choose what you would buy and write a word problem about your purchase. Find the total cost.

_____

_____

Name _____   Date _____

Exploring Multiplication: Partial Products

Find each product using place-value blocks on a mat and the partial product method.

1.	T	O
	1	9
×		8

2.	T	O
	4	6
×		4

3.	H	T	O
	1	2	2
×			5

4.	H	T	O
	2	3	9
×			3

5.	H	T	O
	1	9	3
×			5

MIXED APPLICATIONS

6. Julia's family pays $18 a day to rent skis. How much will they pay for 4 days of ski rentals?

_____

7. A ticket for the ski lift costs $22 per person per day. How much will 3 people pay for ski lift tickets for 4 days?

_____

EVERYDAY MATH CONNECTION

8. Complete the table to show all the different ways you can have $24 using combinations of $10, $5, and $1 bills.

$10 Bill	$5 Bill	$1 Bill	Total
2 × 10 = 20	—	4 × 1 = 4	= $24
			=
			=
			=
			=
			=
			=
			=
			=

Multiplying 3-Digit Numbers

Find the product.

1. 287 × 2	**2.** 114 × 3	**3.** 317 × 3	**4.** 175 × 5	**5.** 224 × 3
6. 182 × 4	**7.** 385 × 2	**8.** 319 × 3	**9.** 136 × 5	**10.** 246 × 4

11. $2 \times 406 =$ _____   **12.** $3 \times 275 =$ _____   **13.** $5 \times 176 =$ _____

14. $3 \times 318 =$ _____   **15.** $4 \times 193 =$ _____   **16.** $4 \times 217 =$ _____

MIXED APPLICATIONS

17. An office building has 135 offices on each floor. How many offices are on 5 floors?

_____

18. There are 248 offices that need 2 lamps and 164 offices that need 1 lamp. How many offices in all need lamps?

_____

NUMBER SENSE

Sometimes you can use mental math to multiply.

Multiply. $4 \times 206 = \square$

Think: $4 \times 6 = 24$

              $4 \times 200 = 800$

              $800 + 24 = 824$

Use mental math to multiply.

19. $6 \times 107 = \square$ **20.** $3 \times 208 = \square$ **21.** $4 \times 205 = \square$

_____   _____   _____

_____   _____   _____

51

Multiplying: More Practice

Find the product.

1.   328
   × 6
	2. 473
	   × 4
		3. 279
		   × 7
			4. 305
			   × 3
				5. 725
				   × 5

6.   458
   × 8
	7. 485
	   × 5
		8. 286
		   × 3
			9. 940
			   × 9
				10. 495
				   × 6

11. $3 \times 534 =$ _____   12. $8 \times 206 =$ _____   13. $7 \times 992 =$ _____

MIXED APPLICATIONS

14. The fair opens at 8:00 A.M. It closes at 11:00 P.M. How many hours a day is the fair open?

15. An adult ticket to the fair costs $4. A child's ticket costs $2. The Alders buy 2 adult tickets and 3 children's tickets. How much do they pay?

16. There are 156 booths at the fair. Three people work at each booth. How many people work at the booths?

17. There are 527 seats in the arena. Shows are given 4 days each week. All the seats are filled. How many people see the show each week?

LOGICAL REASONING

Write the missing digits in the boxes.

18.   3☐
   × 5
   1 6 5

19.   ☐8
   × 9
   3 4 2

20.   2☐
   × 4
   ☐☐8

52

Multiplying Larger Numbers

Estimate. Then use a calculator to find the exact product.

1.	2,096	2.	1,786	3.	4,365	4.	7,258	5.	6,518
	$\times$ 2		$\times$ 4		$\times$ 3		$\times$ 4		$\times$ 7

6. $7 \times 3,624 = $ _____   **7.** $6 \times 4,633 = $ _____

8. $3 \times 7,214 = $ _____   **9.** $8 \times 2,715 = $ _____

MIXED APPLICATIONS

10. The *Morning News* prints 4,750 copies of the newspaper each day. How many newspapers are printed in 5 days?

_____

11. Each delivery truck can be loaded with 1,086 newspapers. How many newspapers can be loaded into 3 trucks?

_____

12. Shana delivers the Sunday papers. She starts her route at 6:15 A.M. and finishes at 7:50 A.M. How long does it take Shana to deliver the Sunday papers?

_____

13. Isaac has 125 customers for Sunday newspaper delivery and 84 customers for weekday delivery. Of the customers who get the Sunday paper, 32 also get the weekday paper. How many customers does Isaac have in all?

_____

WRITER'S CORNER

14. Suppose you are trying to get new customers for your paper route. Write what you would say to people in order to get them to sign up.

_____

_____

_____

Multiplying 3- and 4-Digit Numbers

Estimate each product by rounding. If the estimate is greater than 1,000, find the exact product.

1.	73	2.	36	3.	637	4.	726
	× 2		× 4		× 5		× 8

5.	2,117	6.	538	7.	5,516	8.	5,829
	× 3		× 6		× 7		× 9

Multiply.

9.	73	10.	302	11.	258	12.	4,106
	× 5		× 9		× 2		× 4

13. $7 \times 474 =$ _____

14. $6 \times 4,635 =$ _____

15. $8 \times 1,483 =$ _____

16. $6 \times 357 =$ _____

17. $8 \times 4,251 =$ _____

18. $3 \times 1,975 =$ _____

MIXED APPLICATIONS

19. An airplane is flown 2,200 miles round trip each day for a week. How many miles is that?

_____

20. If a pilot is allowed to fly only 10,000 miles per week, how many pilots are needed to fly the plane in Exercise 19?

_____

MIXED REVIEW

Write two other forms for each number.

21. 2,345

_____

_____

22. forty thousand, ninety-six

_____

_____

Find the sum or difference.

23. $2,615 + 4,394 =$ _____

24. $18,731 - 4,672 =$ _____

Multiples of 10

Complete. Find the value of *n*.

1.
$$50 \times 18 = n$$
$$10 \times \underline{\qquad} \times 18 = n$$
$$10 \times \underline{\qquad} = \underline{\qquad}$$

2.
$$35 \times 40 = n$$
$$35 \times \underline{\qquad} \times 10 = n$$
$$\underline{\qquad} \times 10 = \underline{\qquad}$$

Find the product.

3.
$$52$$
$$\times 30$$

4.
$$23$$
$$\times 50$$

5.
$$15$$
$$\times 20$$

6.
$$32$$
$$\times 30$$

7.
$$41$$
$$\times 60$$

8.
$$36$$
$$\times 40$$

9. $40 \times 54 =$ _____

10. $50 \times 78 =$ _____

11. $80 \times 67 =$ _____

MIXED APPLICATIONS

Use the information in the box to help you answer Exercises 12–16.

How many minutes are there in

12. 12 hours? _____

13. 1 day? _____

| 60 minutes = 1 hour |
| 24 hours = 1 day |

How many hours are there in

14. 1 week? _____

15. 10 days? _____

16. Suppose you sleep 8 hours each night. How many minutes are you awake each day?

_____

WRITER'S CORNER

17. Use the information in the box to write two multiplication questions.

_____

_____

| 60 seconds = 1 minute |
| 60 minutes = 1 hour |

Area Models and Partial Products

Draw a model to represent the product.
Then record the product.

1. 13×42

	40	2
10	400	20
3	120	6

$400 + 20 + 120 + 6 =$ _____

2. 18×34

_____

3. 22×26

_____

4. 15×33

_____

5. 23×29

_____

6. 19×36

_____

PROBLEM SOLVING

7. Sebastian made the following model to find the product 17×24.

	20	4
10	200	40
7	14	28

$200 + 40 + 14 + 28 = 282$

Is his model correct? Explain.

_____

_____

_____

8. Amaryllis bulbs are on sale for 3 for $16.95. Janelle buys 6 bulbs. She gives the clerk two $20 bills. How much change should she receive?

_____

56

Exploring 2-Digit Factors

Multiply using partial products. Then multiply again using the shorter (standard) way.

1. 29	29	**2.** 87	87	**3.** 91	91
$\times$ 66	$\times$ 66	$\times$ 16	$\times$ 16	$\times$ 46	$\times$ 46

MIXED APPLICATIONS

Write a number sentence. Solve.

4. Lui delivers 14 papers on Wood Street. Each paper has 24 pages. How many pages are in all 14 papers?

_____

5. Mr. DeLano ordered newspapers for his class. He ordered 26 papers each day for 19 days. How many newspapers were ordered in all?

_____

MIXED REVIEW

Find the product.

6. $5 \times 60 =$ _____   7. $8 \times 500 =$ _____   8. $4 \times 8,000 =$ _____

9. $7 \times 400 =$ _____   10. $9 \times 3,000 =$ _____   11. $8 \times 900 =$ _____

Complete. Find the value of n.

12. $25 \times 60 = n$

$25 \times$ _____ $\times 10 = n$

_____ $\times 10 =$ _____

13. $35 \times 80 = n$

$35 \times$ _____ $\times 10 = n$

_____ $\times 10 =$ _____

Name _____ Date _____

Multiplying by 2-Digit Numbers

Find the product.

1. 57
× 32

2. 36
× 96

3. 84
× 17

4. 62
× 24

5. 79
× 24

6. 76
× 48

7. 39
× 23

8. 90
× 75

9. 29
× 63

10. 56
× 42

11. $40 \times 78 = n$ _____

12. $42 \times 57 = n$ _____

13. $26 \times 43 = n$ _____

14. $68 \times 46 = n$ _____

MIXED APPLICATIONS

15. A car dealer works 42 hours each week. How many hours does the car dealer work in one year (52 weeks)?

_____

16. Tina drives 18 miles to work. She drives home using the same route. How far does Tina drive in a 21-day work month?

_____

CONSUMER CONNECTION

The fuel economy of a car tells how many miles it can travel on one gallon of gas. The table below lists the fuel economy and tank size for four cars. How far can each vehicle go on one tank of gas?

17. Sunburst _____

18. RX-10 _____

19. TZK-2 _____

20. Delray _____

Model of Car	Fuel Economy (mpg)	Tank Size (in gallons)
Sunburst	32	12
RX-10	36	18
TZK-2	30	24
Delray	28	22

58

Metric Length: cm, dm, m, and km

Circle the most reasonable estimate.

1.

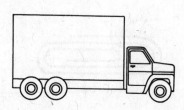

length of a truck
- **a.** 12 m
- **b.** 12 cm
- **c.** 12 km

2.

height of a lamp
- **a.** 3 km
- **b.** 3 m
- **c.** 3 dm

3.

width of a softball
- **a.** 6 m
- **b.** 6 dm
- **c.** 6 cm

Choose the most reasonable unit. Write *cm*, *dm*, *m*, or *km*.

4. height of your desk _____

5. length of a school hallway _____

6. length of a river _____

7. length of a stapler _____

Circle the longer measurement.

8. 5 cm or 5 dm

9. 10 m or 10 dm

10. 16 km or 16 dm

11. 2 m or 2 cm

MIXED APPLICATIONS

12. Jenny runs 7 km a day for 1 week. How many km does she run in that period of time?

_____

13. Enrique has twice as many stickers as Bob. Fay has 8 more stickers than Bob. Roy has 5 fewer stickers than Fay. Roy has 10 stickers. Who has the most stickers?

_____

VISUAL THINKING

14. What is the distance in km from
- **a.** Maple to Elm? _____
- **b.** Elm to Spruce? _____
- **c.** Maple to Spruce if you go through Elm? _____

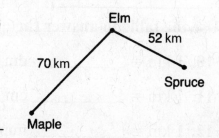

Name _____ Date _____

Metric Length: mm, cm, m, and km

Circle the most reasonable estimate.

1.

height of a tree

  a. 15 km

  b. 15 m

  c. 15 cm

2.

width of a butterfly

  a. 4 mm

  b. 4 m

  c. 4 cm

3.

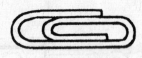

length of a paper clip

  a. 32 m

  b. 32 mm

  c. 32 cm

Choose the most reasonable unit. Write *mm*, *cm*, *m*, or *km*.

4. distance around a school playground _____

5. thickness of a quarter _____

6. length of a pencil _____

7. distance from California to Maine _____

MIXED APPLICATIONS

8. A vine grew 6 cm the first week, 4.3 cm the second week, 5.1 cm the third week, and 7.8 cm the fourth week. How many cm is that?

_____

9. Kelly measures Jack's height to be 4.3 decimeters. Jack measures Kelly's height to be 1.5 meters. Whose measurement is reasonable?

_____

NUMBER SENSE

Use the table to answer the questions.

10. 1 km = _____ dm

11. 1 km = _____ cm

12. 1 km = _____ mm

| 1,000 mm = 1 m |
| 100 cm = 1 m |
| 10 dm = 1 m |
| 1 km = 1,000 m |

Unit 6
Core Skills Math, Grade 4

Length : Customary Units

Choose the most reasonable unit. Write _in._, _ft_, _yd_, or _mi_.

1. The length of an envelope is about 9 _____.

2. The height of a front door is about 8 _____.

3. The width of a car is about 2 _____.

Circle the longer unit.

4. 3 ft or 3 yd   5. 16 ft or 16 in.   6. 23 mi or 23 yd   7. 400 in. or 400 yd

MIXED APPLICATIONS

8. Marvin is 5 feet tall. Mel is 2 yards tall. Who is taller?

   _____

9. Would it be more useful to use a ruler or a yardstick to measure the width of a desk?

   _____

Use the table for Exercises 10–12.

10. Which river is longer than 2,000 miles?

    _____

11. How long is the Snake River?

    _____

Lengths of U.S. Rivers	
River	**Length (in miles)**
Ohio	1,310
Copper	268
Snake	1,040
Mississippi	2,340
Tennessee	886

12. Name the river whose length is about three times the length of the Copper River. _____

SCIENCE CONNECTION

Complete each sentence with the appropriate unit of measure. Write _in._, _ft_, _yd_, or _mi_.

13. A heavy summer rainstorm may bring about 2 _____ of rain.

14. Earth is about 93,000,000 _____ from the sun.

15. The height of a redwood tree may be more than 300 _____.

Capacity: Metric Units

Choose the most reasonable unit. Write _mL_ or _L_.

1. a large bottle of water _____

2. a bowl of soup _____

3. water in a pool _____

4. a small can of juice _____

Circle the more reasonable measure.

5.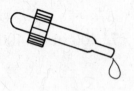

1 mL or 1 L

6.

400 mL or 400 L

7.

15 mL or 15 L

Circle the most reasonable estimate of capacity.

8. A bathtub holds about   **a.** 8 mL   **b.** 80 mL   **c.** 80 L

9. A jar of honey holds about   **a.** 65 mL   **b.** 650 mL   **c.** 65 L

10. A glass of milk holds about   **a.** 400 mL   **b.** 4 L   **c.** 40 L

MIXED APPLICATIONS

11. A tall vase holds about 2 L of water. A wide vase holds about 2,300 mL of water. Which vase holds more water?

_____

12. A large canteen provided each of 4 thirsty hikers with 500 mL of water. How many liters of water did the canteen hold?

_____

LOGICAL REASONING

Circle the measure in each sentence. Change it so it makes sense.

13. Jamie put 350 L of juice into her thermos. _____

14. Maureen put on 200 mL of suntan lotion before going out in the sun. _____

15. Juan poured 2,500 mL of milk into his cereal. _____

16. Mr. Jacobs will use 4 mL of paint to paint his den. _____

Metric Units of Capacity

Circle the more reasonable estimate of capacity.

1. bottle of shampoo   **a.** 300 mL   **b.** 300 L

2. paint bucket   **a.** 2 mL   **b.** 2 L

3. bottle of eye drops   **a.** 15 mL   **b.** 15 L

4. wading pool   **a.** 650 mL   **b.** 650 L

Choose the more reasonable unit of measure. Write *mL* or *L*.

5. fish tank _____   6. cup _____

7. car gas tank _____   8. trash barrel _____

9. thimble _____   10. washing machine _____

MIXED APPLICATIONS

11. Kyle is making lemonade from a powdered mix. The container says 1 scoop of powder will make 0.75 L of lemonade. How many scoops are needed to make 3 L?

    _____

12. Cora is using a glass that holds 250 mL to fill a 4.5-L fishbowl. How many full glasses will she need to fill the fishbowl? (HINT: 4 glasses = 1 liter)

    _____

WRITER'S CORNER

13. Four objects have the following capacities: bowl, 200 mL; bottle of salad dressing, 300 mL; trash can, 5 L; small swimming pool, 250,000 L. Write a problem using this information.

    _____

    _____

    _____

    _____

Exploring Customary Units of Capacity

Choose the most reasonable unit. Write *tbsp*, *c*, *pt*, *qt*, or *gal*.

1.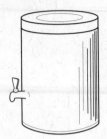

_____

2.

_____

3.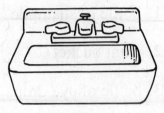

_____

4.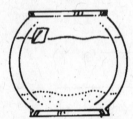

_____

5.

_____

6.

_____

Solve.

7. Jose pours 1 cup of apple juice and 3 cups of grape juice into a large bottle. How many pints of juice are in the bottle?

_____

8. Louise brings a 3-gallon jug of water to share at the tennis match. If each person drinks 1 quart of water, how many people can drink from the jug?

_____

EVERYDAY MATH CONNECTION

When Wanda copied the recipes below, she left out the units of liquid capacity. Use logical reasoning to help you determine a sensible unit for each blank.

9. Fruit Punch — 32 servings

   2 _____ of grape juice

   1 _____ of apple juice

   1 _____ of lemon juice

10. Tomato Noodle Soup — 10 servings

   2 _____ of vegetable broth

   1 _____ of tomato juice

   1 _____ of cooked noodles

Mass: g and kg

Choose the most reasonable unit. Write g or kg.

1.

    _____

2.

    _____

3.

    _____

4.

    _____

5.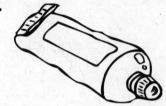

    _____

6.

    _____

Circle the more reasonable estimate of mass.

7. a feather   1 g or 100 g

8. a truck   175 kg or 1,750 kg

9. a pair of socks   20 g or 200 g

10. a piano   40 kg or 450 kg

MIXED APPLICATIONS

11. Pete bought 4 loaves of bread. Each loaf weighs 750 grams. How many kilograms does the bread weigh in all?

    _____

12. Karen needs 1 kilogram of flour. She has 275 grams. How much more flour does Karen need?

    _____

LOGICAL REASONING

13. You need to fill a bag with 14 kg of oranges. How can you measure 14 kg of oranges using a balance scale and these weights: 1 kg, 5 kg, and 10 kg?

    _____

65

Name _____ Date _____

More g and kg

Choose the most reasonable unit. Write *g*, or *kg*.

1. a computer _____

2. a dime _____

3. a cell phone _____

4. a bag of apples _____

Circle the more reasonable estimate of mass.

5.

a. 1 kg   **b.** 1 g

6.

a. 8 kg   **b.** 8 g

MIXED APPLICATIONS

For Exercises 7–10, write how many portions can be made.

7. 50-g portions of cereal _____

8. 15-g portions of raisins _____

9. 5-g portions of raisins _____

10. 75-g portions of coconut _____

11. Three blueberry muffins have a mass of 65 grams.
What is the mass of 3 dozen blueberry muffins? _____

12. Roo Shing can carry 30 kg at once. She has to move 200 kg of rocks.
How many trips must she make? _____

MIXED REVIEW

Find each product.

13.   26
         × 30

14.   48
         × 60

15.   33
         × 20

16.   3,254
         ×   5

17.   65
         × 23

66

Unit 6
Core Skills Math, Grade 4

Weight: Customary Units

Choose the most reasonable unit. Write *oz*, *lb*, or *T*.

1.

_____

2.

_____

3.

_____

4.

_____

5.

_____

6.

_____

Circle the more reasonable estimate of weight.

7.

1 oz or 1 lb

8.

7 lb or 70 lb

9.

5 oz or 25 oz

Complete. You may use a calculator.

10. 5 lb = _____ oz   11. 13 T = _____ lb   12. 64 oz = _____ lb

MIXED APPLICATIONS

13. Harold says his large dog weighs 50. Does he mean pounds, ounces, or tons?

_____

14. Mrs. Ming has six 12-ounce packages of rolls. What is the total weight? Use lb and oz.

_____

EVERYDAY MATH CONNECTION

15. Rose's family recipe for stuffed mushrooms calls for 12 ounces chopped meat to serve 4 people. How many pounds of chopped meat should Rose buy to serve 16 people?

_____

67

The Metric System

Circle the smaller unit of measure.

1. **a.** kilogram
   b. milligram

2. **a.** centimeter
   b. decimeter

3. **a.** liter
   b. milliliter

Circle the larger unit of measure.

4. **a.** gram
   b. milligram

5. **a.** kilometer
   b. millimeter

6. **a.** gram
   b. kilogram

Complete the table.

		km	m	dm	cm	mm
7.	8 m	0.008	8		800	8,000
8.	2 m		2	20	200	2,000
9.	20 m	0.02	20	200		20,000
10.	35 m	0.035	35	350	3,500	

Write each measure using a decimal. Use *m*, *L*, or *g* as the base unit.

11. 3,000 mg = _____

12. 20 mL = _____

13. 600 mm = _____

14. 150 mg = _____

15. 9 cm = _____

MIXED APPLICATIONS

16. Suzanne needs a piece of wire 22 dm long. Joey needs a piece of wire 22 cm long. Who needs the longer piece?

    _____

17. Barbara made a clay sculpture that has a mass of 0.92 kg. Luis wants to make a similar sculpture that is $\frac{1}{10}$ the size of Barbara's. How many grams of clay will he need?

    _____

EVERYDAY MATH CONNECTION

Carlos is painting 8 rooms that are all the same size. He needs 11.4 L of paint for each room.

18. How much paint will he need to paint 4 rooms? _____

19. How much paint will he need to paint all 8 rooms? _____

Patterns in Measurement Units

Each table shows a pattern for two customary units of time or volume.
Label the columns of the table.

1.

_____	_____
1	4
2	8
3	12
4	16
5	20

2.

_____	_____
1	12
2	24
3	36
4	48
5	60

3.

_____	_____
1	2
2	4
3	6
4	8
5	10

4.

_____	_____
1	7
2	14
3	21
4	28
5	35

Use the table for Exercises 5 and 6.

5. Marguerite made the table to compare two metric measures of length. Name a pair of units Marguerite could be comparing.

_____

6. Name another pair of metric units of length that have the same relationship.

_____

?	?
1	10
2	20
3	30
4	40
5	50

WRITER'S CORNER

7. A nonstandard unit is something like a paperclip or a crayon. For example, a desk could have a width of 3 pencils. Write a measurement problem that includes at least one nonstandard measurement.

_____

_____

69

Name _____ Date _____

Mixed Measures

Complete.

1. 8 pounds 4 ounces = _____ ounces

   Think: 8 pounds = 8 × 16 ounces, or _____ ounces.

   128 ounces + 4 ounces = _____ ounces

2. 5 weeks 3 days = _____ days

3. 4 minutes 45 seconds = _____ seconds

4. 4 hours 30 minutes = _____ minutes

5. 3 tons 600 pounds = _____ pounds

6. 6 pints 1 cup = _____ cups

7. 7 pounds 12 ounces = _____ ounces

Add or subtract.

8.   9 gal 1 qt
      + 6 gal 1 qt

9.   12 lb 5 oz
     − 7 lb 10 oz

10.   8 hr 3 min
     + 4 hr 12 min

MIXED APPLICATIONS

11. Michael's basketball team practiced for 2 hours 40 minutes yesterday and 3 hours 15 minutes today. How much longer did the team practice today than yesterday?

    _____

12. Rhonda had a piece of ribbon that was 5 feet 3 inches long. She removed a 5-inch piece to use in her art project. What is the length of the piece of ribbon now?

    _____

EVERYDAY MATH CONNECTION

Name a household item, such as a food or cleaning supply, that is packaged in the following size of container.

13. about 1 liter _____

14. about 250 mL _____

15. about 1 gallon _____

16. about 8 ounces _____

70

Exploring Division: Sharing

Show how many are in each group.

1. Circle 2 equal groups.

How many are in each group? _____

2. Circle 3 equal groups.

How many are in each group? _____

3. Circle 3 equal groups.

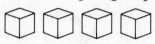
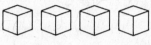
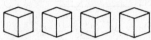

How many are in each group? _____

4. Circle 2 equal groups.

How many are in each group? _____

5. Circle 4 equal groups.

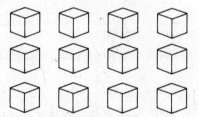

How many are in each group? _____

Decide if you can make 2 equal groups. Circle *Yes* or *No*.

6. 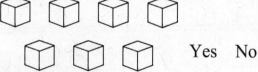 Yes No

7. Yes No

8. Yes No

NUMBER SENSE

9. In a mystery whole number, the digits 1, 2, 3, and 4 are each used once. The least digit is in the tens place. The greatest digit has the least value. The value of the 2 is greater than the value of the 3.

The mystery number is _____.

71

Exploring Division: Separating

Show how many groups.

1. Circle groups of 2.

How many groups? _____

2. Circle groups of 4.

How many groups? _____

3. Circle groups of 3.

How many groups? _____

4. Circle groups of 5.

How many groups? _____

5. How many cars are needed for 16 tires? _____

6. How many bicycles are needed for 12 tires? _____

MIXED REVIEW

7. Write the value of the digit 4 in standard form.

483,503 _____

621,407 _____

742,902 _____

8. What is the *least* number of coins and bills you could receive as change if you pay

for a $7.62 purchase with a $10 bill? _____

Problem-Solving Strategy

DRAW A PICTURE

Draw a picture to represent the problem. Solve.

1. There are 9 fish.
   There are 3 fish in each fishbowl.
   How many fishbowls?

   _____

2. There are 12 pillows.
   There are 4 pillows on each sofa.
   How many sofas?

   _____

   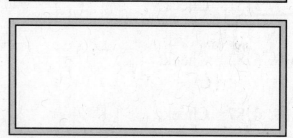

3. There are 15 markers.
   There are 3 markers on each sheet of paper.
   How many sheets of paper?

   _____

   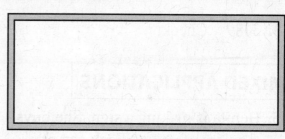

4. There are 28 apples.
   There are 7 apples in each bag.
   How many bags?

   _____

   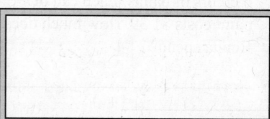

LOGICAL REASONING

Choose the correct answer. Circle *a* or *b*. Then draw a picture to check it.

5. You have 20 sports cards. Which would use more pages in an album?

   a. placing 4 cards on a page

   b. placing 5 cards on a page

Dividing 2-Digit Numbers

Write an X where the first digit in the quotient should be placed. Check by dividing.

1. 6)30   5   Check:

2. 5)85   17   Check:

3. 9)75   8 R 3   Check:

4. 3)82   2   Check:

5. 8)58   7 R 2   Check:
   56

6. 3)27   9   Check:

Find the quotient. Express any remainder as r__. Check by multiplying.

7. 3)51   17   Check:

8. 4)55   13 R 3   Check:
   4
   15
   24

9. 6)82   13 R 4   Check: 6)834

10. 4)96   Check: 25
    13 9
    x 6
    8 34

11. 4)87   21 R 3   Check:
    8
    7

12. 5)65   13   Check:
    5
    15
    00

13. 3)89   29 R 2   Check:
    27
    2

14. 6)71   11 R 5   Check:
    6
    11
    6
    5

MIXED APPLICATIONS

15. Benita is making a sign. She buys 6 colors of paints. Each can of paint costs $1.39. How much does Benita spend? $8.34

16. Benita wants to alternate the paint colors for each letter in her sign. The sign contains 84 letters. How many letters will she have of each color?

NUMBER SENSE

17. Follow the steps using your age. Repeat the problem using ages of other people you know.

> START → Write your age. → Add 3. → Multiply the sum by 3. → Subtract your age. → Subtract 1 more. → Divide by 2. → Subtract your age again. → END

What is the END number every time? _____ 4

9, 12, 36, 27, 26, 13, 4

Dividing 3-Digit Numbers

Write an X where the first digit in the quotient should be placed.

1. $\overset{\text{X}}{4)348}$

2. $\overset{\text{X}}{5)712}$

3. $\overset{\text{X}}{7)948}$

4. $\overset{\text{X}}{4)678}$

5. $\overset{\text{X}}{9)360}$

Find the quotient. Express any remainder as r___. Check by multiplying.

6. $3)254$ Check:

7. $2)130$ Check:

8. $6)737$ Check:

9. $4)419$ Check:

MIXED APPLICATIONS

Gary works at Recycled Audio, a used music store. He arranges tapes, records, and compact discs on shelves. Only one type of audio goes on a shelf. Complete the table. Then use it for Exercises 13 and 14.

	Recycled Audio – Estimated Amount of Audio Material			
	Audio Material	Total Number	Number of Shelves	About How Many per Shelf
10.	Record	487	6	
11.	Tape	944	5	
12.	Compact disc	875	9	

13. Which type of audio material has the fewest items per shelf? __Hard__

14. If the tapes were evenly divided among 8 shelves, how many would be on each shelf? __Hard__

SOCIAL STUDIES CONNECTION

In one scale drawing, every (1 inch) on the drawing represents an actual length of 3 feet. Use division to find the length or height of each object on this scale drawing.

15. 6-ft fence = __2 8__ in.

16. 99-ft boat = __33__ in.

17. 342-ft tree = __4 4__ in.

18. 186-ft bridge = __62__ in.

75

Unit 7
Core Skills Math, Grade 4

Zeros in the Quotient

Write an X where the first digit in the quotient should be placed.

1. 4)216 X

2. 8)578 X

3. 5)602 X

4. 8)824 X

5. 6)6,312 X

Estimate. Then find the quotient. Express any remainder as r__.
Check by multiplying.

6. 7)722   Estimate: ?

7. 4)809   Estimate: ?

8. 8)859   Estimate: ?

Complete. Use mental math to find _n_.

9. If $600 \div 6 = 100$,
then $602 \div 6 = n$.

n = 100 R2

10. If $300 \div 3 = 100$,
then $301 \div 3 = n$.

n = 100 R1

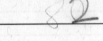

8R2
5)42
40
2

11. If $800 \div 4 = 200$,
then $803 \div 4 = n$.

n = 200 R3

MIXED APPLICATIONS

12. Tami designs covers for compact discs.
She completed 5 covers in 6 weeks.
About how many days does Tami take
to design 1 compact disc cover?

8 2

13. What is the greatest 3-digit number
that gives a 2-digit quotient and
remainder of 1 when divided by 2?

Hard

MIXED REVIEW

Find the quotient. Check by multiplying.

14. $22 \div 4 =$ 5 R

15. $25 \div 4 =$ 6 R1

16. $51 \div 8 =$ 6 R3

Estimate the quotient.

17. 5)42 8R2

18. 6)40 6 R4

19. 9)48 5 R3

20. 8)18 2 R2

21. 7)50 7 R1

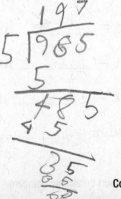

197
5)985
5
485
45
35

Divide by 1-Digit Numbers

Divide and check.

1.
```
    318
  2)636
  - 6↓
    03
  - 2↓
    16
  - 16
     0
```
Check:
```
  318
 ×  2
  636
```

2.
```
   157.7
  4)631.00
   4
   23 1
   20 2 11
   ...
   28
```
Check:

3.
```
  8)906
   88
   26
   24
   20
   16
```
Check:

4.
```
  6)6,739
   6
   739
   72
    9
    8
   10
```
Check:

5.
```
  4)2,328
   20
   328
   32
    8
```
Check:

6.
```
   159.80
  5)7,549
   5
   2549
   25
    49
    45
     40
     40
      0
```
Check:

EVERYDAY MATH CONNECTION

7. The Briggs rented a car for 5 weeks. What was the cost of their rental car per week?

8. The Lees rented a car for 4 weeks. The Santos rented a car for 2 weeks. Whose weekly rental cost was lower? Explain.

Rental Car Costs	
Family	**Total Cost**
Lee	$632
Brigg	$985
Santo	$328

LOGICAL REASONING

9. My quotient is 6 and my divisor is 7. My dividend is 45. I am the remainder. What number am I?

_____

10. If you divide me by 8, my remainder is 7. I am a multiple of 9. What number am I?

_____

Name _____ Date _____

Line Segments, Lines, and Rays

Identify each figure. Write _line segment_, _line_, _point_, or _ray_.

1.   2.   3.   4.

_____ _____ _____ _____

Draw each figure.

5. line *AB*   6. ray *CD*   7. line segment *EF*

Decide whether each figure is a line segment. Write _yes_ or _no_.

8.   9.   10.   11.

_____ _____ _____ _____

MIXED APPLICATIONS

12. Connect the 4 points shown to make a closed figure. Name the figure.

· ·

· ·

_____

13. A football field is 100 yards long. It has numbered lines every ten yards and lines at both ends. How many lines is this? Draw a picture to prove your answer.

_____

VISUAL THINKING

14. Tessa connects all the points in every way possible.

What polygon is formed? _____

What figure is formed inside the polygon?

·

· ·

· ·

_____

Name _____   Date _____

Exploring Angles

Write whether each example is a right, an acute, or an obtuse angle.

1.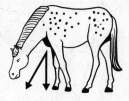

2.

3.

_____   _____   _____

4.

5.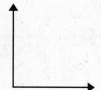

6.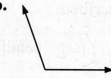

7.

_____   _____   _____   _____

Find the number of acute angles in each letter.

8. V   9. X   10. M   11. Y

_____   _____   _____   _____

MIXED REVIEW

Find each sum or difference.

12.	13.	14.	15.	16.
3,498 + 1,991	89,093 − 13,475	45,079 + 76,809	9,000 − 3,128	24,987 − 8,754

Find the quotient.

17. 4)240   18. 6)879   19. 7)365   20. 8)587   21. 4)864

22. Jason, Ruth, and Kamal have $12.90 to share equally. How much money will each of them get?

23. Beka, Marty, and Henry each earned $7.50 raking leaves. How much did they earn together?

_____   _____

79

Lines and Rays

Write whether each picture suggests *intersecting lines*, *parallel lines*, *perpendicular lines*, or *rays*.

1.

2.

3.

4.

_____   _____   _____   _____

Draw the line segments described.

5. parallel

6. perpendicular

7. intersecting

MIXED APPLICATIONS

8. At what times of the day does the minute hand point to 12 while the hour hand is perpendicular to the minute hand?

_____

9. Martha went ice-skating for 3 hours and 25 minutes. She stopped at 5:15. What time did she begin to skate?

_____

WRITER'S CORNER

Write your own definitions for parallel, perpendicular, and intersecting lines. Ask a family member or friend to identify the word as you read each definition aloud.

10. Parallel lines

11. Perpendicular lines

12. Intersecting lines

_____   _____   _____

_____   _____   _____

Line Relationships

Choose the sentence that describes the relationship of the lines. Circle *a*, *b*, or *c*.

1.

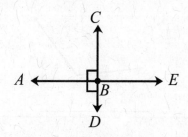

    a. *AB* is parallel to *CD*.

    b. *AB* is perpendicular to *CD*.

    c. *AB* is parallel to *BD*.

2.

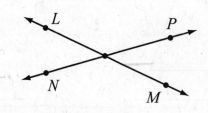

    a. Line *LM* intersects line *NP*.

    b. Line *LM* is perpendicular to line *NP*.

    c. Line *LM* is parallel to line *NP*.

3.

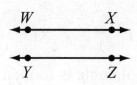

    a. Line *WX* intersects line *YZ*.

    b. Line *WX* is parallel to line *YZ*.

    c. Line *WX* is perpendicular to line *YZ*.

4.

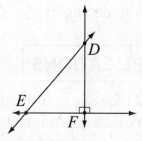

    a. *DE* intersects *EF*.

    b. *DE* is perpendicular to *EF*.

    c. *DE* is parallel to *EF*.

MIXED APPLICATIONS

Use the diagram for Exercises 5–7.

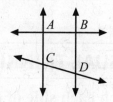

5. Which line is horizontal? _____

6. Which lines are vertical? _____

7. What kind of line relationship do lines *AB* and *BD* represent?

_____

LOGICAL REASONING

8. Without lifting your pencil from the paper, draw 4 line segments that connect all 9 points. Hint: Some of your segments will extend beyond the figure.

Naming Rays and Angles

Identify the angle. Write *right*, *acute*, or *obtuse*.

1.

_____

2.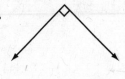

_____

3.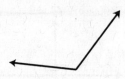

_____

Use the figure for Exercises 4–6.

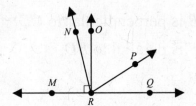

4. Name a right angle. _____

5. Name an obtuse angle. _____

6. Name two acute angles. _____

MIXED APPLICATIONS

7. What kind of angle is formed by the hands of a clock when it is 4:15?

_____

8. What kind of angle is formed by the hands of a clock when it is 9:10?

_____

9. Pietro's pet snake is 256 cm long. His sister's pet snake is 129 cm shorter. How long is his sister's snake?

_____

10. Tara can put 8 photos on each page of her album. She has filled 24 pages and has 64 more photos. How many pages of photos will Tara have filled after putting the 64 photos in the album?

_____

VISUAL THINKING

Match each side of the shapes with a price to find the total cost.

 4¢   5¢   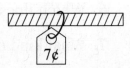 7¢

11.

_____

12.

_____

13.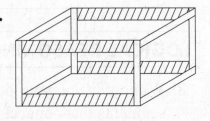

_____

Name _____ Date _____

Name _____ Date _____

Exploring Angle Measurements

Estimate each angle measure. Then use a protractor to measure each angle. You may need to extend the rays.

1. 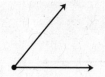   **2.** 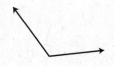   **3.**   **4.**

_____ _____ _____ _____

Use a protractor to draw an angle with the given measurement.

5. 45°   **6.** 90°   **7.** 120°

8. 25°   **9.** 75°   **10.** 145°

VISUAL THINKING

Points are *collinear* if they are on the same line.

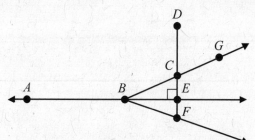

11. Circle each group of points that are collinear.

A, B, E	B, D, E	A, B, C, G
C, G, E	B, C, G	D, C, E, F

Measuring and Constructing Angles

Use a protractor to measure each angle.

1.

2.

3.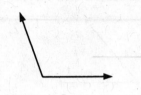

_____ _____ _____

Use a protractor to draw an angle with the given measure.

4. $\angle ABC = 70°$

5. $\angle DEF = 30°$

6. $\angle GHI = 105°$

MIXED APPLICATIONS

Draw a sketch to help you solve Exercises 7 and 8.

7. The sum of the measures of $\angle A$ and $\angle B$ is 180°. $\angle A$ and $\angle C$ have the same measure. If $\angle C$ measures 115°, what is the measure of $\angle B$?

8. When Lynn exercises her dog, she starts walking north. Then she makes three right turns to head home. In what direction is she going?

_____ _____

VISUAL THINKING

9. Study the figure. Then list as many angle names as you can. Give each angle only one name.

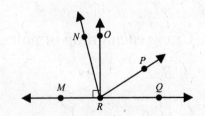

_____

Unit 8
Core Skills Math, Grade 4

Join and Separate Angles

Add to find the measure of the angle. Write an equation to record your work.

1.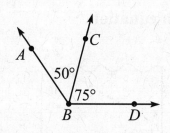

2.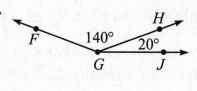

3.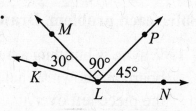

_____   _____   _____

$\angle ABD =$ _____ $\angle FGJ =$ _____ $\angle KLN =$ _____

Use a protractor to find the measure of each angle in the circle.
Measure to the nearest 5 or 10 degrees.

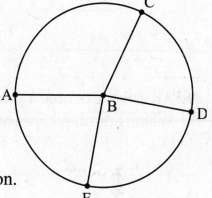

4. $\angle ABC =$ _____   **5.** $\angle DBE =$ _____

6. $\angle CBD =$ _____   **7.** $\angle EBA =$ _____

8. Write the sum of the circle's angle measures as an equation.

_____

Use the design for Exercises 9 and 10.

9. Ned made the design shown. Use a protractor.
Find and write the measure of each of the 3 angles.

_____

10. Write an equation to find the total
measure of the angles.

_____

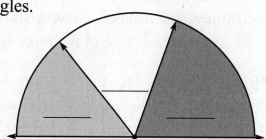

85

Name _____ Date _____

Problem Solving

UNKNOWN ANGLE MEASURES

Solve each problem. Draw a diagram to help. Then write an equation.

1. Wayne is building a birdhouse. He is cutting a board as shown. What is the angle measure, x, of the piece left over?

    Draw a bar model to represent the problem.

    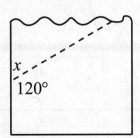

    _____

2. An artist is cutting a piece of metal as shown. What is the angle measure, x, of the piece left over?

    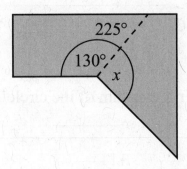

    _____

3. Joan has a piece of material for making a costume. She needs to cut it as shown. What is the angle measure, x, of the piece left over?

    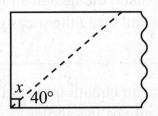

    _____

86

Name _____ Date _____

Basic Ideas of Geometry

Match each description with a geometric figure.
Write _point_, _angle_, _plane_, or _line segment_.

1. intersection of two streets _____

2. piece of cardboard _____

3. flagpole _____

4. head of a pin _____

Use the diagram for Exercises 5 and 6.

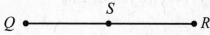

5. Name three points.

6. Name three line segments.

_____

_____

Use the diagram for Exercises 7 and 8.

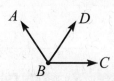

7. Name three rays.

8. Name three angles.

_____

_____

MIXED APPLICATIONS

9. Draw and label line segment _AB_ with ray _AC_.

10. To go home from the park, Melissa walks along a flat sidewalk. Is her path in one plane? Explain.

_____

_____

_____

_____

LOGICAL REASONING

Name the geometric figure described. Make a sketch if it helps.

11. Its middle name is its vertex. _____

12. It is named by its two endpoints. _____

87

Exploring Symmetry

Trace each figure in Exercises 1–3. Then cut out your drawings. Try to fold each one in half so that the two sides match. Write *yes* or *no* to tell whether the figure has a line of symmetry.

1.

_____

2.

_____

3.

_____

Is the dotted line a line of symmetry? Write *yes* or *no*.

4.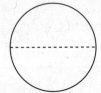

_____

5.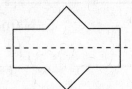

_____

6.

_____

Draw a vertical line of symmetry on each figure.

7.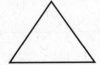

_____

8.

_____

9.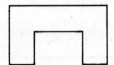

_____

EVERYDAY MATH CONNECTION

Marlise needs to buy 12 pencils. She can buy them separately for $0.80 each or in a box of 6 that costs $4.20.

10. Which should she buy to spend the least amount of money?

_____

11. How much money will she save if she buys the less expensive pencils? Explain your answer.

_____

_____

88

Name _____   Date _____

Understanding Symmetry

How many lines of symmetry does each figure have?

1.

2.

3.

4.

_____   _____   _____   _____

Is the dotted line a line of symmetry?

5.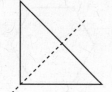

6.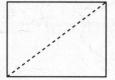

7.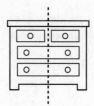

8.

_____   _____   _____   _____

Draw the other half of the figure to make a figure with line symmetry.

9.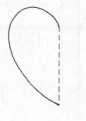

10.

11.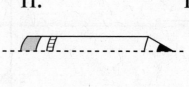

12.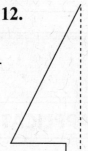

MIXED APPLICATIONS

13. Name three things in your classroom that are symmetric.

    _____

    _____

14. A pilot flew 37,022 miles in May and 40,772 miles in June. How many more miles did the pilot fly in June?

    _____

VISUAL THINKING

15. Imagine you are building a house. You want the front of the house to have a vertical line of symmetry. It must have one door and three windows. The windows may have any shape. Sketch the front of the house.

89

Practice Symmetry

Tell whether the picture shows a mirror image. Write *yes* or *no*.

1.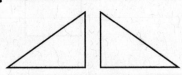

2.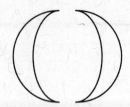

3.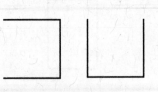

_____   _____   _____

Draw all the lines of symmetry for each figure.

4.

5.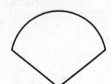

6.

Draw the other half of the figure to make a figure with line symmetry.

7.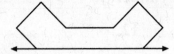

8.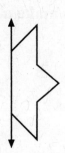

9.

MIXED APPLICATIONS

Use the list of letters for Exercises 10 and 11.

A B C D E F G H I J K L M

10. Which letters have no lines of symmetry? _____

11. Which letters have exactly one line of symmetry? _____

VISUAL THINKING

Here are three different views of the same cube.
The sides are labeled *A*, *B*, *C*, *D*, *E*, and *F*.

12. What letter is opposite the following letters?

E _____   A _____   B _____

90

Unit 9
Core Skills Math, Grade 4

Symmetry in Geometric Figures

Tell whether each figure has line symmetry. Write *yes* or *no*.

1.

2.

3.

4.

_____   _____   _____   _____

Draw all the lines of symmetry.

5.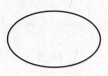

6.

7.

8.

Complete the figures to make figures that have line symmetry.

9.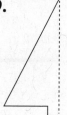

10.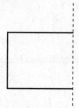

11.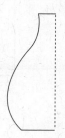

12.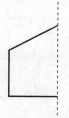

MIXED APPLICATIONS

13. Name two items found outdoors that usually have line symmetry.

_____

_____

14. Shelby says that she used two lines of symmetry to cut a round piece of pita bread into two small and two large pieces. Show how Shelby could cut the pita bread.

LOGICAL REASONING

15. A figure has exactly three lines of symmetry. Draw the figure and all three lines of symmetry.

91

Perimeter

Find the perimeter of the rectangle or square.

1.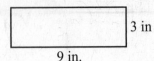

   3 in
   9 in.

   $9 + 3 + 9 + 3 = 24$

   _____ inches

2.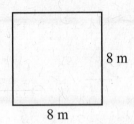

   8 m
   8 m

   _____ meters

3.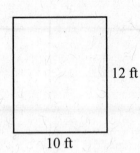

   12 ft
   10 ft

   _____ feet

4.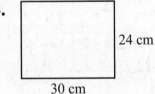

   24 cm
   30 cm

   _____ centimeters

5.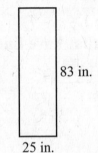

   83 in.
   25 in.

   _____ inches

6.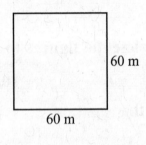

   60 m
   60 m

   _____ meters

EVERYDAY MATH CONNECTION

7. Troy is making a flag shaped like a square. Each side measures 12 inches. He wants to add ribbon along the edges. He has 36 inches of ribbon. Does he have enough ribbon? Make a sketch to help you answer the question.

   _____

8. The width of the Ochoa Community Pool is 20 feet. The length is twice as long as its width. What is the perimeter of the pool?

   _____

9. The perimeter of Jean's rectangular garden is 20 feet. One side measures 6 feet. What are the other side measures?

   _____

Name _____ Date _____

Exploring Area

Draw a model for each given area. Use the grid.

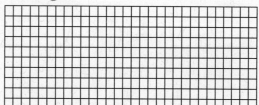

1. 10 square units

2. 16 square units

3. 30 square units

Find the area of the shaded part of the grid in square units. Write a multiplication sentence for Exercises 4 and 5.

4. 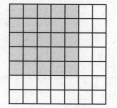 **5.** 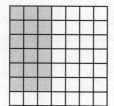 **6.** 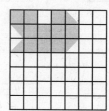 **7.**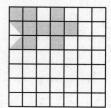

_____ _____ _____ _____

_____ _____

Use the figures for Exercises 8 and 9.

A. 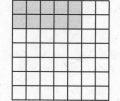 **B.** 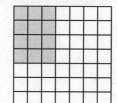 **C.** 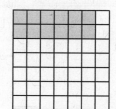 **D.**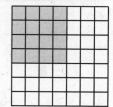

8. Which of the figures have the same area but different perimeters?

_____

9. Which of the figures have the same perimeters but different areas?

_____

SOCIAL STUDIES CONNECTION

Some states are almost rectangular in shape. Use a calculator to find the area of these states.

10.
Colorado

L: 600 km W: 450 km

Area = _____

11.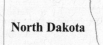
North Dakota

L: 540 km W: 330 km

Area = _____

93

Unit 9
Core Skills Math, Grade 4

Area

Use the area formula to find the area of the rectangle or square.

1. 12 ft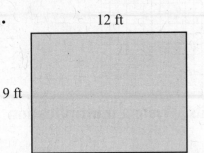
9 ft

_____

2. 8 yd
8 yd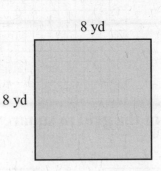

_____

3. 15 m
3 m

_____

4. 13 in.
6 in.

_____

5. 30 cm
5 cm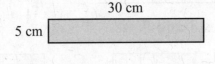

_____

6. 14 ft
4 ft

_____

EVERYDAY MATH CONNECTION

7. Meghan is putting wallpaper on a wall that measures 8 feet by 12 feet. How much wallpaper does Meghan need to cover the wall?

_____

8. Bryson is laying down sod in his yard. Each piece of sod is a 1-foot by 1-foot square. How many pieces of sod will Bryson need to cover his yard if his yard measures 30 feet by 14 feet?

_____

94

Area of Combined Rectangles

Find the area of the combined rectangles.

1.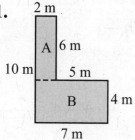

2.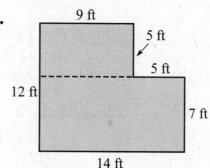

3.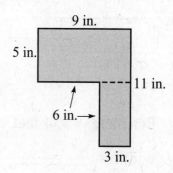

_____ _____ _____

Divide each figure into two rectangles. Then find the area of the figures.

4.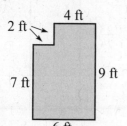

5.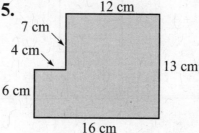

6.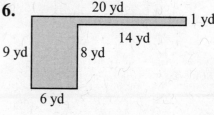

_____ _____ _____

Use the diagram for Exercises 7–9.

The diagram below represents the counter space Nadia wants to build in her craft room.

7. Find the two missing measures.
Width (*w*) of Scrapbooking: 15 − 11 = _____
Length of Painting: 9 − *w* = _____

8. What is the area of the space that Nadia has shown for scrapbooking?

_____

9. What is the area of the space she has shown for painting?

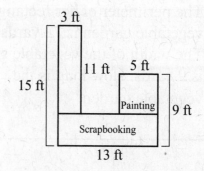

_____

95

Name _____ Date _____

Find Unknown Measures

Find the unknown measure of the rectangle.

1.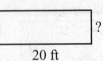

20 ft

Perimeter = 54 feet

width = _____

Think: $P = (2 \times l) + (2 \times w)$
$54 = (2 \times 20) + (2 \times w)$
$54 = 40 + (2 \times w)$

Since $54 = 40 + 14$, $2 \times w = 14$, and $w = 7$.

2.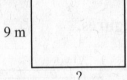

9 m

?

Perimeter = 42 meters

length = _____

3.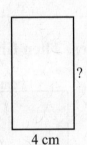

?

4 cm

Area = 28 square centimeters

height = _____

4.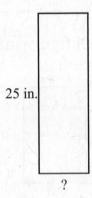

25 in.

?

Area = 200 square inches

base = _____

EVERYDAY MATH CONNECTION

5. Susie is an organic vegetable grower. The perimeter of her rectangular vegetable garden is 72 yards. The width of the vegetable garden is 9 yards. How long is the vegetable garden?

_____

6. An artist is creating a rectangular mural for the Northfield Community Center. The mural is 7 feet tall and has an area of 84 square feet. What is the length of the mural?

_____

Classify Quadrilaterals

Classify each figure as many ways as possible. Write *quadrilateral*, *trapezoid*, *parallelogram*, *rhombus*, *rectangle*, or *square*.

1.

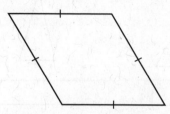

Think: _____ pairs of parallel sides

_____ sides of equal length

_____ right angles

_____

_____

2.

_____

_____

_____

3.

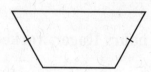

_____

_____

_____

4.

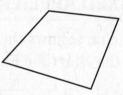

_____

_____

_____

5.

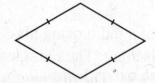

_____

_____

_____

6.

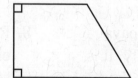

_____

_____

_____

7.

_____

_____

_____

LOGICAL REASONING

8. Alan drew a polygon with four sides and four angles. All four sides are equal. None of the angles are right angles. What figure did Alan draw?

_____

9. Teresa drew a quadrilateral with 2 pairs of parallel sides and 4 right angles. What quadrilaterals could she have drawn?

_____

Classifying Triangles

Name each triangle based on the lengths of its sides. Write: *equilateral*, *scalene*, or *isosceles*.

1. 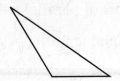 _____

2. _____

3. 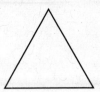 _____

4. _____

MIXED APPLICATIONS

The chart shows the number of hours Roger worked this week.
Use the chart for Exercises 5–8.

Sun	Mon	Tues	Wed	Thurs	Fri	Sat
12–4	12–8	1–4	Off	Off	1–9	9–5

5. How many hours did Roger work?

_____

6. If Roger earns $10 per hour, how much did he earn?

_____

7. The store where Roger works pays about $20 an hour for electricity. It is open from 10 A.M. to 9 P.M. six days a week. What is the store's weekly electric bill?

_____

8. Roger bought a radio using his employee discount. The radio usually sells for $129.95. The discount was $12.99. How much did Roger pay for the radio?

_____

LOGICAL REASONING

Multiply using mental math.

9. $100 \times 84 = 8{,}400$, so

$50 \times 84 =$ _____

10. $100 \times 28 = 2{,}800$, so

$50 \times 28 =$ _____

11. $100 \times 44 = 4{,}400$, so

$25 \times 44 =$ _____

12. $100 \times 88 = 8{,}800$, so

$25 \times 88 =$ _____

Angles in a Triangle

Name each triangle based on the size of its angles. Write: *right*, *acute* or *obtuse*.

1.   2. 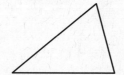   3. 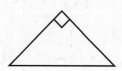   4.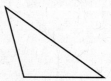

_____   _____   _____   _____

MIXED APPLICATIONS

5. The playground at Molly's school is in the shape of an equilateral triangle. The playground at David's school is in the shape of an acute triangle. Could Molly and David go to the same school? Explain.

_____

_____

6. Ace Parking Garage charges $1 for the first hour of parking and 50¢ for every hour after that. Terry parks his car in the garage for 9 hours. How much will he have to pay for parking?

_____

_____

7. Ace Parking Garage has 1,125 parking spaces. There are 745 cars parked. How many empty spaces are there?

_____

8. A playground is in the shape of a regular polygon. If it has five sides, what is its shape?

_____

MIXED REVIEW

9. Estimate 45×56 using front-end estimation. _____

10. Estimate 45×56 using rounding. _____

Add, subtract, or multiply.

11. 12.04	12. 38.60	13. 6,008	14. 35	15. 19.70	16. 23.40	17. 36,721	18. 128
28.30	− 12.92	− 2,419	× 76	+ 8.93	− 9.75	− 29,879	× 57
+ 16.15							

Name _____ Date _____

Degrees

Tell the measure of the angle in degrees.

1.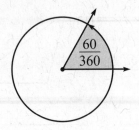

2.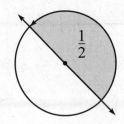

3.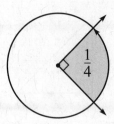

_____ _____ _____

Classify the angle. Write *acute*, *obtuse*, *right*, or *straight*.

4.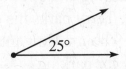

5.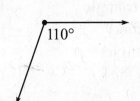

6.

_____ _____ _____

Classify the triangle. Write *acute*, *obtuse*, or *right*.

7.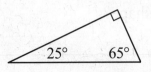

8.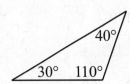

9.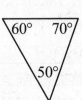

_____ _____ _____

Ann started reading at 4:00 P.M. and finished at 4:20 P.M.

10. Through what fraction of a circle did
the *minute* hand turn?

_____

11. How many degrees did the *minute* hand turn?

_____

Start   End

100

Unit 9
Core Skills Math, Grade 4

Finding a Fraction of a Number

Use the pictures to help you complete Exercises 1–3.

1.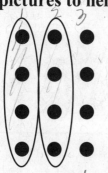

   $\frac{2}{3}$ of 12 = _____ 6

   $\frac{24}{3}$

2.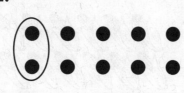

   $\frac{1}{5}$ of _____ = 2

   10

3.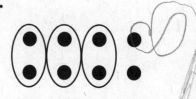

   $\frac{6}{8}$ of 8 = 6

Complete. Use multiplication or division to help you.

4. $\frac{1}{4}$ of 8 = _____ 2

5. $\frac{5}{6}$ of 12 = _____ 6

6. $\frac{1}{3}$ of 9 = _____ 3

7. $\frac{2}{5}$ of 25 = _____ 5

8. $\frac{2}{3}$ of 18 = _____ 6

9. $\frac{1}{8}$ of 24 = _____ 3

10. Velma has 18 baseball cards. One half show National League players. How many of Velma's cards show National League players?

    _____ 9

11. Samuru has a collection of 15 model cars. Three-fifths are sports cars. How many of his cars are sports cars?

    _____ 5

12. Ramona has a collection of 80 stamps. One-fourth are British stamps. The rest are U.S. stamps. How many of Ramona's stamps are U.S. stamps?

    _____ 20

13. Brett's display case can hold 4 rows of rocks with 12 rocks in each row. The case is $\frac{5}{8}$ full. How many rocks are displayed in the case?

    _____ 3

CONSUMER CONNECTION

The hobby shop is having a sale on stamp albums. $\frac{1}{3}$ of $15 = $5. You save $5. Write the amount saved.

STAMP ALBUMS
Regularly $15
NOW $\frac{1}{3}$ OFF!

14. Regular Price: $9 $\frac{1}{3}$ off   _____ 3$

15. Regular Price: $24 $\frac{1}{2}$ off   _____ 12$

16. Regular Price: $20 $\frac{2}{5}$ off   _____ 10$

Name _____ 4 _____ Date _____

Finding Part of a Group

Circle $\frac{1}{3}$ of each group. Write a number sentence to show the answer.
(Use counters if they are helpful.)

1.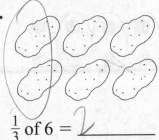

$\frac{1}{3}$ of 6 = _2__

2.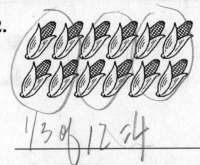

1/3 of 12 = 4

3.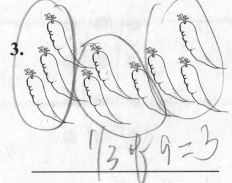

1/3 of 9 = 3

Find $\frac{1}{5}$ of each group. Write a number sentence to show the answer.

4.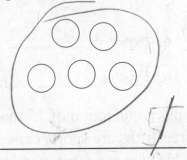

___1___

5.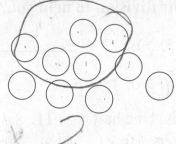

___2___

6.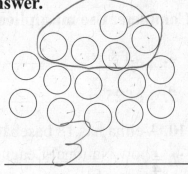

___3___

MIXED APPLICATIONS

7. Ruth has $4. She spent $\frac{1}{2}$ of her money on lunch. How much money did she have left?

2$

8. Sam bought 24 apples. He used $\frac{1}{4}$ of them to make an apple pie. How many apples did Sam use?

6

VISUAL THINKING

9. How many circles are in the group? __12__

Find the number of circles in

$\frac{1}{3}$ of the group ___4_____

$\frac{2}{3}$ of the group ___6_____

$\frac{1}{4}$ of the group ___3_____

$\frac{3}{4}$ of the group _____

102

Exploring Equivalent Fractions

Complete these equivalent fractions. Use fraction bars or counters to help you.

1. $\frac{1}{3} = \frac{\boxed{2}}{6}$ 2. $\frac{1}{2} = \frac{\boxed{2}}{4}$ 3. $\frac{3}{4} = \frac{\boxed{6}}{8}$ 4. $\frac{3}{9} = \frac{\boxed{1}}{3}$

Look at the first figure in Exercises 5 and 6. Circle the figure that shows an equivalent fraction.

5.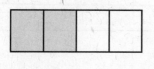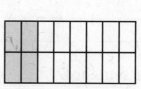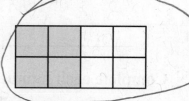

6.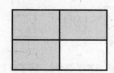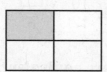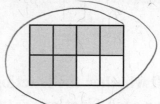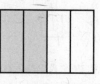

Write two equivalent fractions for each fraction.

7. $\frac{1}{4}$ ___2/8 4/16___ 8. $\frac{1}{3}$ ___2/10 4/20___   9. $\frac{2}{3}$ ___4/6 6/18___ 10. $\frac{3}{8}$ ___9/24 6/16___

MIXED APPLICATIONS

11. Alex eats $\frac{2}{8}$ of a muffin. His brother eats $\frac{1}{4}$ of the same muffin. Compare the amounts they eat.

same
they both ate same amount

12. Lena uses $\frac{1}{4}$ of a dozen eggs to make an omelet. How many eggs does she use?

___3___

VISUAL THINKING

Write four equivalent fractions for the shaded part of each figure.

13.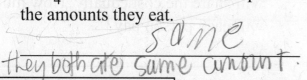

12/36

4/12   6/18

8/24   9/19   12/36

14.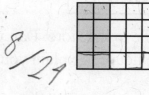

8/24

4/12   1/3   2/6

3/9

Name _____ Date _____

Equivalent Fractions

Write a fraction that names the shaded part.

1.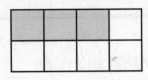

2.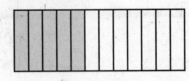

3.

$3/8$ $5/12$ $2/6$

Complete each number sentence.

4. $\frac{3}{6} = \frac{15}{\boxed{10}}$ 5. $\frac{7}{8} = \frac{\boxed{21}}{24}$ 6. $\frac{10}{12} = \frac{\boxed{5}}{6}$ 7. $\frac{35}{100} = \frac{7}{\boxed{20}}$

Write *yes* or *no* to tell whether the fractions are equivalent. If they are not, write an equivalent fraction for each fraction.

8. $\frac{3}{4}, \frac{15}{20}$ _____yes_____   9. $\frac{2}{6}, \frac{4}{18}$ _NO_   10. $\frac{2}{5}, \frac{4}{12}$ ___yes___   11. $\frac{6}{8}, \frac{9}{12}$ __no__

MIXED APPLICATIONS

12. Cory answered 6 out of 8 questions correctly on his last quiz. The next quiz has 24 questions. How many questions must he answer correctly to get the same score?

    3 questions

13. A pizza costs \$12. Jan and 5 friends will share the cost equally. How much will each person pay?

    2 12/6

LOGICAL REASONING

14. Josh walks $\frac{5}{8}$ mile to the store. Dan walks $\frac{10}{16}$ mile to the same store. Do Josh and Dan live in the same house? Explain your answer.

    yes because mitiply 5 and 8. That
    equals 10 and 16. so 5/8 = 10/16
    and they live in the same
    hoensc

104

Name _____ Date _____

Compare Fractions Using Models

Write the fraction for each figure. Then compare using <, >, or =.

1.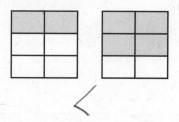

2.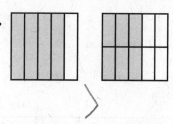

3.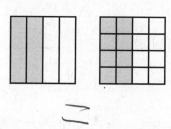

Write *like* or *unlike* to describe each pair of fractions. The compare using <, >, or =.
You may use fraction bars to help you.

4. $\frac{1}{4}$ ⟨ $\frac{2}{4}$ *unlike*   5. $\frac{1}{2}$ = $\frac{2}{4}$ *like*   6. $\frac{4}{10}$ < $\frac{9}{10}$ *unlike*

7. $\frac{4}{5}$ > $\frac{3}{5}$ *unlike*   8. $\frac{2}{6}$ < $\frac{2}{3}$ *unlike*   9. $\frac{2}{4}$ > $\frac{2}{6}$ *unlike*

Place each set in order from least to greatest. Use equivalent fractions if you need to.

10. $\frac{6}{10}, \frac{4}{10}, \frac{9}{10}$ _____ $\frac{4}{10}, \frac{6}{10}, \frac{9}{10}$

11. $\frac{1}{2}, \frac{5}{6}, \frac{1}{6}, \frac{2}{3}$ _____ $\frac{1}{6}, \frac{1}{2}, \frac{2}{3}, \frac{5}{6}$

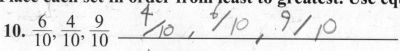

MIXED APPLICATIONS

12. Ming Lei used $\frac{2}{3}$ cup of raisins in her raisin bread. Elizabeth used $\frac{5}{8}$ cup raisins in her raisin bread. Which girl used more raisins?

_____ 2/3

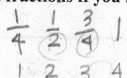

13. Of the 20 cookbooks in the school library, 5 are dessert books. In simplest form, what fraction of the cookbooks are dessert books? $\frac{5}{20} \div \frac{5}{5} = \frac{1}{4}$

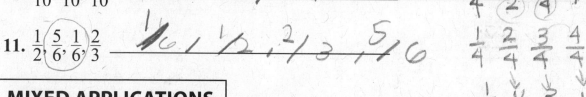

NUMBER SENSE

Compare. Write <, >, or =.

14. $\frac{1}{2}$ of 4 = $\frac{1}{3}$ of 6 $\frac{4}{2}$

15. $\frac{1}{3}$ of 12 < $\frac{1}{2}$ of 10

16. $\frac{5}{7}$ of 7 > $\frac{1}{3}$ of 9

17. $\frac{1}{4}$ of 8 < $\frac{1}{2}$ of 6

105

Compare Fractions Using Benchmarks

Use a benchmark fraction such as $\frac{1}{4}$, $\frac{1}{2}$, or $\frac{3}{4}$ to compare. Write < or >.

1. $\frac{1}{8}$ ⊘ $\frac{6}{10}$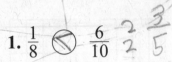

2. $\frac{4}{12}$ ⦸ $\frac{4}{6}$

3. $\frac{2}{8}$ ⦸ $\frac{1}{2}$

4. $\frac{3}{5}$ ⦸ $\frac{3}{3}$

5. $\frac{7}{8}$ ⦸ $\frac{5}{10}$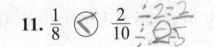

6. $\frac{9}{12}$ ⦸ $\frac{1}{3}$

7. $\frac{4}{6}$ ⦸ $\frac{7}{8}$

8. $\frac{2}{4}$ ⦸ $\frac{2}{3}$

9. $\frac{3}{5}$ ⦸ $\frac{1}{4}$

10. $\frac{6}{10}$ ⦸ $\frac{2}{5}$

11. $\frac{1}{8}$ ⦸ $\frac{2}{10}$

12. $\frac{2}{3}$ ⦸ $\frac{5}{12}$

13. $\frac{4}{5}$ ⦸ $\frac{5}{6}$

14. $\frac{3}{5}$ ⦸ $\frac{5}{8}$

15. $\frac{8}{8}$ ⦸ $\frac{3}{4}$

MIXED APPLICATIONS

16. Erika ran $\frac{3}{8}$ mile. Maria ran $\frac{3}{4}$ mile. Who ran farther? Explain how to use a benchmark fraction to answer the question.

   Maria ran fardier beease in fractions less the deminatonor bigger the peace

17. Carlos finished $\frac{1}{3}$ of his art project on Monday. Tyler finished $\frac{1}{2}$ of his art project on Monday. Who finished more of his art project on Monday?

   $\frac{1}{2}$

Name _____ Date _____

Compare Two Fractions

Compare. Write <, >, or =.

1. $\frac{1}{3}$ ◯ $\frac{2}{6}$ 2. $\frac{1}{3}$ ◯ $\frac{2}{2}$ 3. $\frac{2}{3}$ ◯ $\frac{5}{6}$ 4. $\frac{5}{6}$ ◯ $\frac{3}{4}$

5. $\frac{2}{4}$ ◯ $\frac{3}{4}$ 6. $\frac{1}{2}$ ◯ $\frac{3}{6}$ 7. $\frac{1}{2}$ ◯ $\frac{3}{8}$ 8. $\frac{6}{8}$ ◯ $\frac{3}{4}$

9. $\frac{3}{8}$ ◯ $\frac{4}{16}$ 10. $\frac{2}{5}$ ◯ $\frac{4}{10}$ 11. $\frac{4}{5}$ ◯ $\frac{3}{5}$ 12. $\frac{5}{6}$ ◯ $\frac{1}{2}$

MIXED APPLICATIONS

13. Barry used $\frac{3}{4}$ bag of fertilizer on his apple trees. He used $\frac{7}{8}$ bag on his pear trees. On which trees did he use more fertilizer?

Pear trees

14. Rob made some fruit sauce. He used $\frac{3}{5}$ cup of strawberries and $\frac{7}{10}$ cup of blueberries. Did he use a greater amount of strawberries or blueberries?

blueberries

15. A $\frac{3}{5}$-quart bottle of apple juice costs $3. A $\frac{7}{8}$-quart bottle of apple juice costs $3. Which bottle is the better buy?

7/8 a quart of apple juice

16. Write a question in which the fractions $\frac{1}{3}$ and $\frac{3}{5}$ are compared.

Which is grater 1/3 3/5 juice

NUMBER SENSE

Write two fractions greater than the one shown.

17. $\frac{1}{2}$ _____

18. $\frac{3}{4}$ _____

19. $\frac{1}{8}$ _____

20. $\frac{3}{5}$ _____

21. $\frac{1}{6}$ _____

22. $\frac{7}{8}$ _____

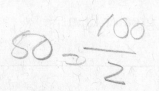
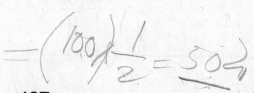

107

Name _____   Date _____

Compare and Order Fractions

Compare. Use < or >.

1. $\frac{1}{4}$ ◯ $\frac{3}{8}$ 2. $\frac{1}{3}$ ◯ $\frac{5}{6}$ 3. $\frac{3}{4}$ ◯ $\frac{5}{12}$ 4. $\frac{1}{5}$ ◯ $\frac{2}{25}$

5. $\frac{3}{7}$ ◯ $\frac{2}{5}$ 6. $\frac{5}{6}$ ◯ $\frac{2}{9}$ 7. $\frac{1}{10}$ ◯ $\frac{2}{15}$ 8. $\frac{5}{8}$ ◯ $\frac{7}{12}$

Use <, >, or = to compare the fractions.

9. $\frac{3}{5}$ ◯ $\frac{4}{5}$ 10. $\frac{2}{3}$ ◯ $\frac{3}{5}$ 11. $\frac{4}{6}$ ◯ $\frac{5}{12}$ 12. $\frac{3}{12}$ ◯ $\frac{3}{4}$

13. $\frac{5}{8}$ ◯ $\frac{9}{16}$ 14. $\frac{5}{10}$ ◯ $\frac{3}{6}$ 15. $\frac{3}{8}$ ◯ $\frac{6}{16}$ 16. $\frac{75}{100}$ ◯ $\frac{25}{50}$

Use < to compare the fractions from least to greatest.

17. $\frac{3}{5}, \frac{2}{15}, \frac{1}{5}$ _____   18. $\frac{2}{3}, \frac{3}{4}, \frac{1}{8}$ _____   19. $\frac{2}{5}, \frac{2}{3}, \frac{1}{2}$ _____

20. $\frac{5}{6}, \frac{2}{3}, \frac{3}{8}$ _____   21. $\frac{1}{3}, \frac{1}{2}, \frac{5}{9}$ _____   22. $\frac{2}{6}, \frac{3}{12}, \frac{3}{4}$ _____

MIXED APPLICATIONS

23. On the same science test, three students answered the following fractions of the questions correctly: Ana $-\frac{2}{3}$, Jesse $-\frac{5}{6}$, and Alan $-\frac{3}{4}$. Which student answered the most questions correctly?

_____

24. Candidate A received $\frac{3}{8}$ of the votes. Candidate B received $\frac{5}{16}$ of the votes. Were there only two candidates in the election? Explain.

_____

_____

NUMBER SENSE

Use like fractions to answer each question.

25. Name a fraction that is greater than $\frac{3}{5}$ but less than $\frac{9}{10}$.

_____

26. Name a fraction that is less than $\frac{3}{4}$ but greater than $\frac{5}{12}$.

_____

Unit 10
Core Skills Math, Grade 4

Exploring Mixed Numbers

Write a mixed number for each picture.

1.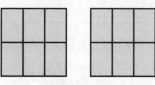

2.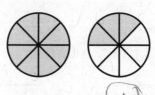

3.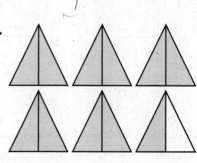

_____   _____   _____

Write each fraction as a mixed number. You may use your fraction circles to help you.

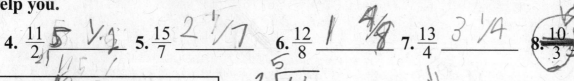

4. $\frac{11}{2}$ _____   5. $\frac{15}{7}$ _____   6. $\frac{12}{8}$ _____   7. $\frac{13}{4}$ _____   8. $\frac{10}{3}$ _____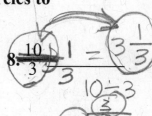

MIXED APPLICATIONS

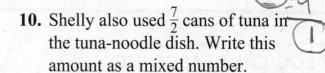

9. Shelly used $\frac{11}{3}$ cups of noodles to make a tuna-noodle dish. Write this amount as a mixed number.

_____

10. Shelly also used $\frac{7}{2}$ cans of tuna in the tuna-noodle dish. Write this amount as a mixed number.

_____

11. Shelly paid $5.95 for 4 cans of tuna and a bag of noodles. Each can of tuna cost $1.29. How much did the noodles cost?

_____

12. A cup is 8 ounces of liquid. Shelly used 30 ounces of milk to make some bread. How many cups did she use?

_____

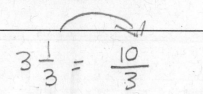

LOGICAL REASONING

Complete each pattern. Think: What fraction is added to find the next number?

13. $\frac{1}{2}$, 1, $1\frac{1}{2}$, _____, _____, _____, _____

14. $\frac{2}{3}$, 1, $1\frac{1}{3}$, _____, _____, _____, _____

15. $\frac{4}{7}$, 1, $1\frac{3}{7}$, _____, _____, _____, _____

Rename Fractions and Mixed Numbers

Write the mixed number as an improper fraction.

1. $2\frac{3}{5}$ **2.** $4\frac{1}{3}$ **3.** $1\frac{2}{5}$ **4.** $3\frac{2}{3}$

_____   _____   _____   _____

5. $4\frac{1}{8}$ **6.** $1\frac{7}{10}$ **7.** $5\frac{1}{2}$ **8.** $2\frac{3}{8}$

_____   _____   _____   _____

Write the improper fraction as a mixed number.

9. $\frac{31}{6}$ **10.** $\frac{20}{10}$ **11.** $\frac{15}{8}$ **12.** $\frac{13}{6}$

_____   _____   _____   _____

13. $\frac{23}{10}$ **14.** $\frac{19}{5}$ **15.** $\frac{11}{3}$ **16.** $\frac{9}{2}$

_____   _____   _____   _____

LOGICAL REASONING

17. A recipe calls for $2\frac{2}{4}$ cups of raisins, but Julie has only a $\frac{1}{4}$-cup measuring cup. How can she use this measuring cup to measure out the raisins?

_____

18. If Julie needs $3\frac{1}{4}$ cups of oatmeal, how many $\frac{1}{4}$ cups of oatmeal will she use?

_____

110

Write Fractions as Sums

Write the fraction as a sum of unit fractions.

1. $\frac{4}{5} = $ _____

   Think: Add $\frac{1}{5}$ four times.

2. $\frac{3}{8} = $ _____

3. $\frac{6}{12} = $ _____

4. $\frac{4}{4} = $ _____

Write the fraction as a sum of fractions three different ways.

5. $\frac{7}{10}$

_____

_____

_____

6. $\frac{6}{6}$

_____

_____

_____

LOGICAL REASONING

7. Miguel's teacher asks him to color $\frac{4}{8}$ of his grid. He must use 3 colors: red, blue, and green. There must be more green sections than red sections. How can Miguel color the sections of his grid to follow all the rules?

_____

_____

8. Petra is asked to color $\frac{6}{6}$ of her grid. She must use 3 colors: blue, red, and pink. There must be more blue sections than red sections or pink sections. What are the different ways Petra can color the sections of her grid and follow all the rules?

_____

_____

_____

111

Multiples of Unit Fractions

Write the fraction as a product of a whole number and a unit fraction.

1. $\frac{5}{6} =$ _____

2. $\frac{7}{8} =$ _____

3. $\frac{5}{3} =$ _____

4. $\frac{9}{10} =$ _____

5. $\frac{3}{4} =$ _____

6. $\frac{11}{12} =$ _____

7. $\frac{4}{6} =$ _____

8. $\frac{8}{20} =$ _____

9. $\frac{13}{100} =$ _____

List the next four multiples of the unit fraction.

10. $\frac{1}{5}$, _____, _____, _____, _____

11. $\frac{1}{8}$, _____, _____, _____, _____

MIXED APPLICATIONS

12. So far, Monica has read $\frac{5}{6}$ of a book. She has read the same number of pages each day for 5 days. What fraction of the book does Monica read each day?

_____

13. Nicholas buys $\frac{3}{8}$ pound of cheese. He puts the same amount of cheese on 3 sandwiches. How much cheese does Nicholas put on each sandwich?

_____

Multiples of Fractions

List the next four multiples of the fraction.

1. $\frac{3}{5}$, _____, _____, _____, _____

2. $\frac{2}{6}$, _____, _____, _____, _____

3. $\frac{4}{8}$, _____, _____, _____, _____

4. $\frac{5}{10}$, _____, _____, _____, _____

Write the product as the product of a whole number and a unit fraction.

5.

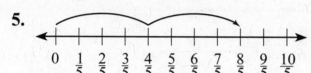

$2 \times \frac{4}{5} =$ _____

6.

$5 \times \frac{2}{3} =$ _____

MIXED APPLICATIONS

7. Jessica is making 2 loaves of banana bread. She needs $\frac{3}{4}$ cup of sugar for each loaf. Her measuring cup can hold only $\frac{1}{4}$ cup of sugar. How many times will Jessica need to fill the measuring cup in order to get enough sugar for both loaves of bread?

   _____

8. A group of four students is performing an experiment with salt. Each student must add $\frac{3}{8}$ teaspoon of salt to a solution. The group has only a $\frac{1}{8}$-teaspoon measuring spoon. How many times will the group need to fill the measuring spoon in order to perform the experiment?

   _____

Name _____ Date _____

Add Fractions Using Models

Find the sum. Use fraction strips to help.

1. $\frac{2}{6} + \frac{1}{6} =$ _____

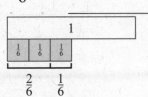

2. $\frac{4}{10} + \frac{5}{10} =$ _____

3. $\frac{1}{3} + \frac{2}{3} =$ _____

4. $\frac{2}{4} + \frac{1}{4} =$ _____

5. $\frac{2}{12} + \frac{4}{12} =$ _____

6. $\frac{1}{6} + \frac{2}{6} =$ _____

7. $\frac{3}{12} + \frac{9}{12} =$ _____

8. $\frac{3}{8} + \frac{4}{8} =$ _____

9. $\frac{3}{4} + \frac{1}{4} =$ _____

10. $\frac{1}{5} + \frac{2}{5} =$ _____

MIXED APPLICATIONS

11. Lola walks $\frac{4}{10}$ mile to her friend's house. Then she walks $\frac{5}{10}$ mile to the store. How far does she walk in all?

_____

12. Evan eats $\frac{1}{8}$ of a pan of lasagna and his brother eats $\frac{2}{8}$ of it. What fraction of the pan of lasagna do they eat in all?

_____

13. Jacqueline buys $\frac{2}{4}$ yard of green ribbon and $\frac{1}{4}$ yard of pink ribbon. How many yards of ribbon does she buy in all?

_____

14. Shu mixes $\frac{2}{3}$ pound of peanuts with $\frac{1}{3}$ pound of almonds. How many pounds of nuts does Shu mix in all?

_____

Exploring Adding Fractions with Like Denominators

Use fraction circles to find the sum. You may write the sum in simplest form.

1.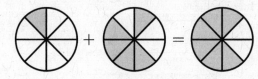

2.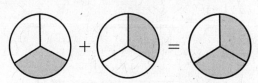

$\frac{1}{8} + \frac{5}{8} = \frac{\square}{\square}$

$\frac{1}{3} + \frac{1}{3} = \frac{\square}{\square}$

3. $\frac{1}{8} + \frac{4}{8} = \frac{\square}{\square}$

4. $\frac{3}{10} + \frac{6}{10} = \frac{\square}{\square}$

5. $\frac{1}{6} + \frac{4}{6} = \frac{\square}{\square}$

6. $\frac{1}{3} + \frac{2}{3} = \frac{\square}{\square}$

7. $\frac{2}{4} + \frac{1}{4} = \frac{\square}{\square}$

8. $\frac{4}{8} + \frac{3}{8} = \frac{\square}{\square}$

9. $\frac{3}{5} + \frac{1}{5} = \frac{\square}{\square}$

10. $\frac{1}{10} + \frac{7}{10} = \frac{\square}{\square}$

MIXED APPLICATIONS

11. A scout troop hiked along a trail. The scouts hiked $\frac{2}{8}$ of the way on the first day and $\frac{3}{8}$ of the way on the second day. What fraction of the trail did they hike?

_____

12. Of the scout troop, $\frac{3}{12}$ slept in one tent and $\frac{4}{12}$ slept in another. The rest slept in a cabin. What fraction of the troop slept in tents?

_____

NUMBER SENSE

Write the missing addend.

13. $\frac{4}{5} +$ _____ $= 1$

14. $\frac{2}{3} +$ _____ $= 1$

15. $\frac{4}{10} +$ _____ $= 1$

Subtract Fractions Using Models

Subtract. Use fraction strips to help.

1. $\dfrac{4}{5} - \dfrac{1}{5} =$ _____

1
$\frac{1}{5}$	$\frac{1}{5}$	$\frac{1}{5}$	$\frac{1}{5}$ →

2. $\dfrac{3}{4} - \dfrac{1}{4} =$ _____

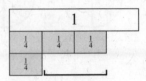

3. $\dfrac{5}{6} - \dfrac{1}{6} =$ _____

4. $\dfrac{7}{8} - \dfrac{1}{8} =$ _____

5. $1 - \dfrac{2}{3} =$ _____

6. $\dfrac{8}{10} - \dfrac{2}{10} =$ _____

7. $\dfrac{3}{4} - \dfrac{1}{4} =$ _____

8. $\dfrac{7}{6} - \dfrac{5}{6} =$ _____

EVERYDAY MATH CONNECTION

Use the table for Exercises 9 and 10.

9. Ena is making trail mix. She buys the items shown in the table. How many more pounds of pretzels than raisins does she buy?

_____

10. How many more pounds of granola than banana chips does she buy?

_____

Item	Weight (in pounds)
Pretzels	$\frac{7}{8}$
Peanuts	$\frac{4}{8}$
Raisins	$\frac{2}{8}$
Banana Chips	$\frac{3}{8}$
Granola	$\frac{5}{8}$

Exploring Subtracting Fractions with Like Denominators

Use fraction models to find the difference.
You may write the difference in simplest form.

1. 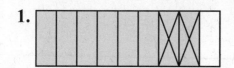   2. [shaded fraction model]   3.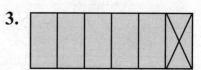

$\frac{8}{9} - \frac{2}{9} =$ _____ $\frac{3}{4} - \frac{2}{4} =$ _____ $\frac{6}{6} - \frac{1}{6} =$ _____

4. $\frac{3}{4} - \frac{2}{4} = \frac{\boxed{}}{4}$ 5. $\frac{3}{3} - \frac{2}{3} = \frac{\boxed{}}{3}$ 6. $\frac{5}{10} - \frac{4}{10} = \frac{\boxed{}}{10}$ 7. $\frac{3}{5} - \frac{1}{5} = \frac{\boxed{}}{5}$

8. $\frac{7}{8} - \frac{2}{8} = \frac{\boxed{}}{8}$ 9. $\frac{5}{6} - \frac{4}{6} = \frac{\boxed{}}{6}$ 10. $\frac{9}{10} - \frac{2}{10} = \frac{\boxed{}}{10}$ 11. $\frac{6}{8} - \frac{3}{8} = \frac{\boxed{}}{8}$

12. $\begin{array}{r} \frac{7}{7} \\ -\frac{2}{7} \\ \hline \end{array}$ 13. $\begin{array}{r} \frac{10}{11} \\ -\frac{4}{11} \\ \hline \end{array}$ 14. $\begin{array}{r} \frac{7}{9} \\ -\frac{4}{9} \\ \hline \end{array}$ 15. $\begin{array}{r} \frac{5}{5} \\ -\frac{3}{5} \\ \hline \end{array}$ 16. $\begin{array}{r} \frac{9}{12} \\ -\frac{3}{12} \\ \hline \end{array}$ 17. $\begin{array}{r} \frac{6}{7} \\ -\frac{2}{7} \\ \hline \end{array}$

MIXED APPLICATIONS

18. Elena had $\frac{5}{6}$ of a box of pancake mix. She used $\frac{4}{6}$ of the box to make pancakes for breakfast. How much of the pancake mix was left?

_____

19. Elena had $\frac{4}{5}$ of a pitcher of orange juice. Her family drank $\frac{3}{5}$ of a pitcher of the juice. Was there almost no orange juice left, $\frac{1}{2}$ pitcher left, or a whole pitcher left?

_____

NUMBER SENSE

20. Tom subtracted a fraction from $\frac{11}{12}$. The answer in simplest form was $\frac{1}{2}$. What fraction did he subtract?

_____

Add and Subtract Fractions Using Models

Find the sum or difference. Use fraction strips to help.

1. $\dfrac{4}{12} + \dfrac{8}{12} =$ _____

2. $\dfrac{3}{6} - \dfrac{1}{6} =$ _____

3. $\dfrac{4}{5} - \dfrac{3}{5} =$ _____

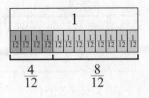

4. $\dfrac{6}{10} + \dfrac{3}{10} =$ _____

5. $1 - \dfrac{3}{8} =$ _____

6. $\dfrac{1}{4} + \dfrac{2}{4} =$ _____

7. $\dfrac{9}{12} - \dfrac{5}{12} =$ _____

8. $\dfrac{5}{6} - \dfrac{2}{6} =$ _____

9. $\dfrac{2}{3} + \dfrac{1}{3} =$ _____

EVERYDAY MATH CONNECTION

Use the table for Exercises 10 and 11.

10. Guy finds how far his house is from several locations and makes the table shown. How much farther away from Guy's house is the library than the cafe?

_____

11. If Guy walks from his house to school and back, how far does he walk?

_____

Distance from Guy's House	
Location	**Distance (in miles)**
Library	$\dfrac{9}{10}$
School	$\dfrac{5}{10}$
Store	$\dfrac{7}{10}$
Cafe	$\dfrac{4}{10}$
Yogurt Shop	$\dfrac{6}{10}$

Add and Subtract Like Fractions Vertically

Write an addition or subtraction sentence for each model.

1.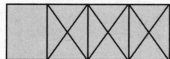

2.

3.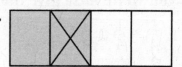

_____   _____   _____

Find the sum or difference. You may write the answer in simplest form.

4. $\dfrac{4}{8}$
   $+\dfrac{3}{8}$

5. $\dfrac{3}{6}$
   $+\dfrac{1}{6}$

6. $\dfrac{6}{8}$
   $+\dfrac{1}{8}$

7. $\dfrac{7}{10}$
   $-\dfrac{2}{10}$

8. $\dfrac{2}{4}$
   $+\dfrac{1}{4}$

9. $\dfrac{4}{6}$
   $-\dfrac{1}{6}$

10. $\dfrac{3}{5}$
   $-\dfrac{1}{5}$

11. $\dfrac{9}{10}$
   $-\dfrac{1}{10}$

12. $\dfrac{3}{6}$
   $+\dfrac{2}{6}$

13. $\dfrac{5}{8}$
   $-\dfrac{1}{8}$

MIXED APPLICATIONS

14. Pablo read for $\dfrac{5}{12}$ of an hour on Monday and $\dfrac{7}{12}$ of an hour on Tuesday. How many hours did he read on these two days?

_____

15. Some students belong to the art club. Of these students, $\dfrac{1}{3}$ are in the third grade, $\dfrac{1}{2}$ are in the fourth grade, and $\dfrac{1}{6}$ are in the fifth grade. Which grade has the most students in the art club?

_____

NUMBER SENSE

Write the missing addend.

16. $\dfrac{3}{8} + \dfrac{\square}{\square} = 1$

17. $\dfrac{\square}{\square} + \dfrac{2}{7} = 1$

18. $\dfrac{\square}{\square} + \dfrac{91}{100} = 1$

Add and Subtract Like Fractions Horizontally

Tell whether the sum or difference in simplest form is correct. Write *true* or *false*. If you write *false* give the correct answer.

1. $\frac{1}{4} + \frac{1}{4} \overset{?}{=} \frac{3}{4}$ _____

2. $\frac{5}{8} - \frac{3}{8} \overset{?}{=} \frac{1}{4}$ _____

3. $\frac{5}{12} + \frac{1}{12} \overset{?}{=} \frac{1}{3}$ _____

4. $\frac{5}{6} - \frac{3}{6} \overset{?}{=} \frac{2}{3}$ _____

Find the sum or difference. You may write your answer in simplest form.

5. $\frac{3}{5} + \frac{1}{5} =$ _____

6. $\frac{3}{10} + \frac{2}{10} =$ _____

7. $\frac{4}{12} - \frac{2}{12} =$ _____

8. $\frac{3}{8} + \frac{4}{8} =$ _____

9. $\frac{4}{6} - \frac{2}{6} =$ _____

10. $\frac{8}{12} + \frac{1}{12} =$ _____

11. $\frac{5}{8} - \frac{3}{8} =$ _____

12. $\frac{4}{10} - \frac{1}{10} =$ _____

MIXED APPLICATIONS

13. Dina lives $\frac{9}{10}$ mile from school. She has ridden her bike $\frac{4}{10}$ mile. How much farther does she have to ride?

_____

14. Riley used $\frac{1}{4}$ teaspoon of salt and $\frac{1}{8}$ teaspoon of pepper in his salad dressing. How much salt and pepper did he use?

_____

MIXED REVIEW

Use a benchmark fraction to help you choose the better estimate. Circle *a* or *b*.

15. $\frac{2}{3} + \frac{4}{5}$ a. $1\frac{1}{2}$ b. 2

16. $\frac{5}{6} - \frac{3}{8}$ a. 1   b. $\frac{1}{2}$

17. $\frac{3}{5} + \frac{3}{4}$ a. $1\frac{1}{2}$ b. 2

Find the product.

18. $\begin{array}{r} 472 \\ \times 35 \\ \hline \end{array}$

19. $\begin{array}{r} 284 \\ \times 62 \\ \hline \end{array}$

20. $\begin{array}{r} 602 \\ \times 47 \\ \hline \end{array}$

21. $\begin{array}{r} 197 \\ \times 29 \\ \hline \end{array}$

Addition and Subtraction of Fractions with Like Denominators

Find each sum or difference. Write the answer in simplest form.

1. $\dfrac{1}{8}$
    $+\dfrac{3}{8}$

2. $\dfrac{1}{5}$
    $+\dfrac{2}{5}$

3. $\dfrac{3}{4}$
    $+\dfrac{1}{4}$

4. $\dfrac{7}{10}$
    $+\dfrac{1}{10}$

5. $\dfrac{9}{10}$
    $+\dfrac{3}{10}$

6. $\dfrac{5}{6}$
    $-\dfrac{3}{6}$

7. $\dfrac{11}{12}$
    $-\dfrac{5}{12}$

8. $\dfrac{7}{8}$
    $-\dfrac{1}{8}$

9. $\dfrac{5}{10}$
    $-\dfrac{3}{10}$

10. $\dfrac{9}{10}$
    $-\dfrac{3}{10}$

MIXED APPLICATIONS

11. Jen has $\dfrac{11}{12}$ yard of fabric. She used $\dfrac{7}{12}$ yard of it on a project. How much fabric is left?

_____

12. Over three days, Kevin's town received these amounts of rain: $\dfrac{7}{10}$ in., $\dfrac{3}{10}$ in., and $\dfrac{5}{10}$ in. How much rain is this in three days?

_____

NUMBER SENSE

A music store has these instruments on display: 10 guitars, 20 drums, and 5 violins.

13. What is the total number of instruments on display?

_____

14. What fraction of the instruments on display are guitars? Write the fraction in simplest form. Explain what the fraction means.

_____

_____

15. What fraction of the instruments are not guitars?

_____

Finding a Common Denominator

Use fraction strips to help you find a common denominator for each fraction pair.

1. $\frac{2}{5}$ and $\frac{7}{10}$ _____

2. $\frac{2}{3}$ and $\frac{5}{6}$ _____

3. $\frac{1}{2}$ and $\frac{3}{4}$ _____

4. $\frac{1}{6}$ and $\frac{5}{12}$ _____

5. $\frac{1}{2}$ and $\frac{3}{5}$ _____

6. $\frac{3}{8}$ and $\frac{1}{4}$ _____

MIXED APPLICATIONS

7. Samantha mowed $\frac{4}{6}$ of the front lawn after breakfast. She took a break and then mowed $\frac{1}{6}$ of the lawn. How much of the lawn has she mowed?

_____

8. Barney watered the lawn for $\frac{1}{3}$ hour in the afternoon and $\frac{2}{3}$ hour in the evening. How many minutes did he spend watering the yard? Explain.

_____

VISUAL THINKING

Draw hands on each clock face so you can shade an area of it that matches the given fraction. For example, a clock that shows 5:00 could represent $\frac{5}{12}$ or $\frac{7}{12}$.

$\frac{5}{12}$

$\frac{7}{12}$

9. $\frac{1}{2}$

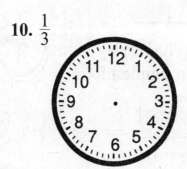

10. $\frac{1}{3}$

11. $\frac{1}{4}$

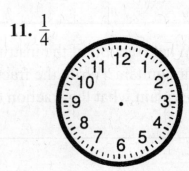

Name _____

Name _____   Date _____

Adding and Subtracting Mixed Numbers

Find the sum or difference. You may write your answer in simplest form.

1.

$5\frac{5}{8} - 2\frac{3}{8} =$ _____

2. $1\frac{3}{10}$ **3.** $7\frac{5}{6}$ **4.** $8\frac{3}{4}$ **5.** $2\frac{1}{4}$ **6.** $2\frac{3}{5}$ **7.** $3\frac{3}{6}$
$+ 3\frac{4}{10}$ $- 1\frac{4}{6}$ $- 2\frac{1}{4}$ $+ 2\frac{2}{4}$ $+ 2\frac{1}{5}$ $- 1\frac{1}{6}$
_____   _____   _____   _____   _____   _____

MIXED APPLICATIONS

Use the table to answer Exercises 8 and 9.

8. What is the combined length of
Elm Trail and Cherry Trail?

_____

9. How much longer is Apple Trail
than Maple Trail?

_____

Bike Trails in Bamboo Park	
Trail	**Length (in miles)**
Cherry Trail	$1\frac{1}{8}$
Apple Trail	$2\frac{5}{8}$
Elm Trail	$\frac{6}{8}$
Oak Trail	$3\frac{7}{8}$
Maple Trail	$2\frac{4}{8}$

SPORTS CONNECTION

10. A $2\frac{2}{3}$-miles bicycle race is held on a $\frac{1}{3}$-mile track. Use subtraction to find the number
of laps around the track the racers must go to complete the race.

_____

Subtracting Mixed Numbers with Like Denominators

Find the difference. Write the answer in simplest form.

1. $15\frac{4}{5}$
   $- 2\frac{1}{5}$

2. $18\frac{5}{12}$
   $- 3\frac{1}{12}$

3. $12\frac{3}{5}$
   $- 5\frac{2}{5}$

4. $17\frac{5}{6}$
   $- 9\frac{1}{6}$

5. $11\frac{7}{8}$
   $- 9\frac{3}{8}$

Find the difference. You may need to rename the whole number.
Write the answer in simplest form.

6. $8\frac{3}{5}$
   $- 5\frac{4}{5}$

7. 6
   $- 4\frac{10}{12}$

8. $6\frac{5}{12}$
   $- 3\frac{7}{12}$

9. $9\frac{2}{5}$
   $- 5\frac{3}{5}$

10. $3\frac{1}{5}$
    $- 1\frac{3}{5}$

11. $6\frac{1}{4}$
    $- 4\frac{3}{4}$

12. $5\frac{1}{8}$
    $- 2\frac{3}{8}$

13. $14\frac{1}{3}$
    $- 8\frac{2}{3}$

14. $10\frac{3}{5}$
    $- 6\frac{4}{5}$

15. 8
    $- 3\frac{7}{10}$

MIXED APPLICATIONS

16. Larry is running a $6\frac{1}{4}$-mile race. He has already run $2\frac{3}{4}$ miles. How many more miles does he have to run to finish the race?

_____

17. Jena used $5\frac{7}{8}$ jars of blue paint and $3\frac{3}{8}$ jars of green paint to paint a mural. How many more jars of blue paint than green paint did she use?

_____

NUMBER SENSE

Look at the fractions in each pattern. Find the pattern. Write the next two numbers in each pattern.

18. $2\frac{3}{4}$, $2\frac{1}{2}$, $2\frac{1}{4}$, 2, _____, _____

19. 6, $5\frac{2}{3}$, $5\frac{1}{3}$, 5, _____, _____

Problem Solving

MULTISTEP FRACTION PROBLEMS

Read each problem and solve. You may use fraction strips or a sketch to help you.

1. Each child in the Smith family was given an orange cut into 8 equal sections. Each child ate $\frac{5}{8}$ of the orange. After combining the leftover sections, Mrs. Smith noted that there were exactly 3 full oranges left. How many children are in the Smith family?

   _____

2. Val walks $2\frac{3}{5}$ miles each day. Bill runs 10 miles once every 4 days. In 4 days, who covers the greater distance?

   _____

3. Chad buys peanuts in 2-pound bags. He repackages them into bags that hold $\frac{5}{6}$ pound of peanuts. How many 2-pound bags of peanuts should Chad buy so that he can fill the $\frac{5}{6}$-pound bags without having any peanuts left over?

   _____

4. A carpenter has several boards of equal length. He cuts $\frac{3}{5}$ of each board. After cutting the boards, the carpenter notices that he has enough pieces left over to make up the same length as 4 of the original boards. How many boards did the carpenter start with?

125

Name _____ Date _____

Multiply a Fraction by a Whole Number Using Models

Multiply. Write the answer as an improper fraction.

1. $2 \times \dfrac{5}{6} =$ _____

2. $3 \times \dfrac{2}{5} =$ _____

3. $7 \times \dfrac{3}{10} =$ _____

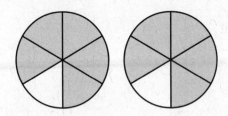

4. $3 \times \dfrac{5}{12} =$ _____

5. $6 \times \dfrac{3}{4} =$ _____

6. $4 \times \dfrac{2}{8} =$ _____

7. $5 \times \dfrac{2}{3} =$ _____

8. $2 \times \dfrac{7}{8} =$ _____

9. $6 \times \dfrac{4}{5} =$ _____

EVERYDAY MATH CONNECTION

10. Matthew walks $\dfrac{5}{8}$ mile to the bus stop each morning. How far will he walk in 5 days?

_____

11. Emily uses $\dfrac{2}{3}$ cup of milk to make one batch of muffins. How many cups of milk will Emily use if she makes 3 batches of muffins?

_____

Multiply a Fraction or Mixed Number by a Whole Number

Multiply. Write the product as a mixed number in simplest form.

1. $5 \times \frac{3}{10} =$ _____

2. $3 \times \frac{3}{5} =$ _____

3. $5 \times \frac{3}{4} =$ _____

Write the mixed number as a fraction. Then multiply.

4. $4 \times 1\frac{1}{5} =$ _____

5. $2 \times 2\frac{1}{3} =$ _____

6. $5 \times 1\frac{1}{6} =$ _____

7. $2 \times 2\frac{7}{8} =$ _____

8. $7 \times 1\frac{3}{4} =$ _____

9. $8 \times 1\frac{3}{5} =$ _____

10. Brielle exercises for $\frac{3}{4}$ hour each day for 6 days in a row. Altogether, how many hours does she exercise during the 6 days?

_____

11. A recipe for quinoa calls for $2\frac{2}{3}$ cups of milk. Conner wants to make 4 batches of quinoa. How much milk does he need?

_____

LANGUAGE ARTS CONNECTION

Newspaper headlines use both exact and rounded numbers. Read each headline. Tell if the number is most likely _exact_ or _rounded_.

12. Transit System $300,000 in Debt _____

13. Company Sold for $5.2 Million _____

14. Concert Over Sold – 28 Receive Refund _____

15. Temperature Reaches 108.5° _____

127

Problem Solving

COMPARISON PROBLEMS WITH FRACTIONS

Read each problem and solve. Draw a picture of the problem to help you.

1. A shrub is $1\frac{2}{3}$ feet tall. A small tree is 3 times as tall as the shrub. How tall is the tree?

   _____

2. You run $1\frac{3}{4}$ miles each day. Your friend runs 4 times as far as you do. How far does your friend run each day?

   _____

3. At the grocery store, Ayla buys $1\frac{1}{3}$ pounds of ground turkey. Tasha buys 2 times as much ground turkey as Ayla. How much ground turkey does Tasha buy?

   _____

4. When Nathan's mother drives him to school, it takes $\frac{1}{5}$ hour. When Nathan walks to school, it takes him 4 times as long to get to school. How long does it take Nathan to walk to school?

   _____

Line Plots

1. Some students compared the time they spend riding the school bus. Complete the tally table and line plot to show the data.

Time Spent on School Bus	
Time (in hours)	**Tally**
$\frac{1}{6}$	I I

Time Spent on School Bus (in hours)
$\frac{1}{6}$, $\frac{3}{6}$, $\frac{4}{6}$, $\frac{2}{6}$, $\frac{3}{6}$, $\frac{1}{6}$, $\frac{3}{6}$, $\frac{3}{6}$

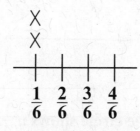

Time Spent on School Bus (in hours)

Use your line plot for Exercises 2 and 3.

2. How many students compared times? _____

3. What is the difference between the longest time and shortest time students spent riding the bus? _____

For Exercises 4 and 5, make a tally table on a separate sheet of paper. Make a line plot in the space below the problem.

4.
Milk Bought at Lunch (in quarts)
$\frac{1}{8}$, $\frac{2}{8}$, $\frac{2}{8}$, $\frac{4}{8}$, $\frac{1}{8}$, $\frac{3}{8}$, $\frac{4}{8}$, $\frac{2}{8}$, $\frac{3}{8}$, $\frac{2}{8}$

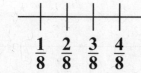

Milk Bought at Lunch (in quarts)

5.
Distance Between Stops for a Rural Mail Carrier (in miles)
$\frac{3}{10}$, $\frac{4}{10}$, $\frac{5}{10}$, $\frac{1}{10}$, $\frac{5}{10}$, $\frac{4}{10}$, $\frac{4}{10}$, $\frac{3}{10}$

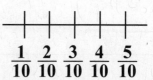

Distance Between Stops for a Rural Mail Carrier (in miles)

Angles and Fractional Parts of a Circle

Tell what fraction of the circle the shaded angle represents.

1.

2.

3.

_____   _____   _____

Tell whether the angle on the circle shows a $\frac{1}{4}$, $\frac{1}{2}$, $\frac{3}{4}$, or 1 full turn clockwise or counterclockwise.

4.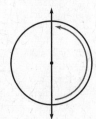

5.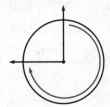

6.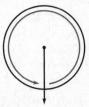

_____   _____   _____

7. Shelley exercised for 15 minutes. Describe the turn the minute hand made.

Start   End

8. Mark took 30 minutes to finish lunch. Describe the turn the minute hand made.

Start   End

_____

_____

_____

_____

Decimals: Tenths

Write the decimal that names the part that is shaded.

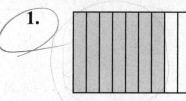

1. 0.7

2. 0.7

3. 0.4

Write each fraction as a decimal.

4. $\frac{2}{10} =$ 0.20

5. $\frac{5}{10} =$ 0.5

6. $\frac{9}{10} =$ 0.9

7. $\frac{3}{10} =$ 0.3

Write each decimal as a fraction.

8. $0.4 = \frac{4}{10}$

9. $0.8 = \frac{8}{10}$

10. $0.1 = \frac{1}{10}$

11. $0.6 = \frac{6}{10}$

MIXED APPLICATIONS

Write the answer as a fraction and a decimal.

12. In one tennis match, Chris won 6 out of 10 games. What part of the games did Chris win?

0.6

13. Jamie served the ball 10 times. He scored a point on his serve 3 of those times. On what part of his serves did Jamie score a point?

0.3

NUMBER SENSE

14. Write each number as a decimal. Then order the decimals from least to greatest.

$\frac{3}{10}$ 0.3 $\frac{2}{10}$ 0.2 seven tenths 0.7 five tenths 0.5

0.2 _____ 0.3 _____ 0.5 _____ 0.7
least   greatest

Name _____ Date _____

Decimals: Hundredths

Write the decimal that names the part that is shaded.

1. 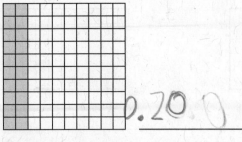 0.20

2. 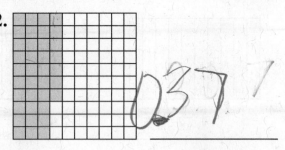 037

Write each fraction as a decimal.

3. $\frac{83}{100} =$ 0.83

4. $\frac{48}{100} =$ 0.48

5. $\frac{9}{100} =$ 0.9

Write each decimal as an amount of money.

6. forty-five hundredths 0.45

7. sixty-two hundredths 0.62

Use the place-value chart for Exercises 8 and 9.

8. In 0.56, what digit is in the hundredths place? _____ 6

9. In 0.34, in what place is the digit 0? _____ ones

Ones	.	Tenths	Hundredths
0	.	5	6
0	.	3	4

MIXED APPLICATIONS

10. Marcy spent 60 cents on a pen and 10 cents on an eraser. Write the amount she spent as a decimal and as a dollar amount.

0.70

11. Charlie had 100 squiggle pencils to sell. He sold 30 of them. Write the part of the pencils he sold as a fraction and as a decimal.

0.30 $\frac{30}{100}$

LOGICAL REASONING

12. Complete the heading on the place-value chart to name the decimal parts of a dollar.

Dollars	Dimes	Pennies
$1.	0	0

Unit 12
Core Skills Math, Grade 4

Name _____ Date _____

Decimals Greater Than 1

Write the decimal that names the part that is shaded.

1.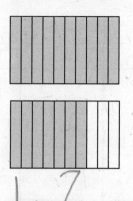

    1.7

2.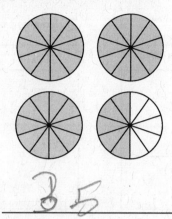

    3 5

3.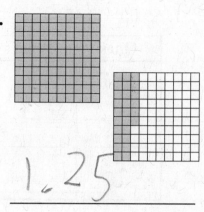

    1.25

Write each mixed number as a decimal.

4. $6\frac{7}{10}$ = 6.7

5. $12\frac{72}{100}$ = 12.72

6. $27\frac{4}{100}$ = 27.04

Write each decimal as a mixed number.

7. 4.3 = 4 $\frac{0}{10}$

8. 9.03 = 9 $\frac{3}{100}$

9. 67.29 = 67 $\frac{29}{100}$

Write each decimal in words.

10. 4.7 _____

11. 8.92 _____

MIXED APPLICATIONS

12. Freda bought a toy bat and ball for $3.17. The bat cost $1.98. How much did the ball cost?

    1.19

    $$\begin{array}{r} 2\ 10 \\ \cancel{3}.\cancel{1}7 \\ -1.98 \\ \hline 1.19 \end{array}$$

13. Susan and Jeff each had a dollar. Susan spent $\frac{2}{5}$ of her dollar. Jeff spent $\frac{7}{10}$ of his dollar. Who spent more?

    Jeff

WRITER'S CORNER

14. Shade the grids to show that 0.3 = 0.30. Explain why the two decimals represent the same part of a whole.

    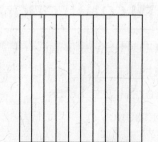 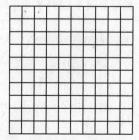

    _____

    _____

Exploring Subtraction and Money

Write each problem on the place-value chart. Then find the difference.

1. $9.00 − 3.45 = \underline{\hspace{2cm}}$

Ones	10ths	100ths
9	0	0
3	4	5
5	5	5

2. $48.01 − 29.34 = \underline{\hspace{2cm}}$

Tens	Ones	10ths	100ths
3 4 2	7 8 9	9 0 3	11 1 4
1	8	6	7

3. $24.36 − 9.57 = \underline{\hspace{2cm}}$

$9 9 = \$9.00$

Tens	Ones	10ths	100ths
2	4	3	6
	9	5	7
1	4	7	9

$+M−27.35$
$T−12.86$

Circle the number sentence that will answer the question. Then solve.

4. Arlo spent $46.85 on a jacket. He gave the clerk $50.00. How much change did Arlo get?

   a. $46.85 + $50.00 = ☐

   b. $50.00 + $46.85 = ☐

   (c.) $50.00 − $46.85 = ☑

5. Mrs. Chow paid $27.35 for groceries on Monday and $12.86 on Tuesday. How much did she spend?

   a. $27.35 − $12.86 = ☐

   b. $27.35 + $12.86 = ☐

   c. $27.35 + ☐ = $12.86

EVERYDAY MATH CONNECTION

6. Tyrone has $3.00. He wants to buy three stickers for $0.65 and a sticker book for $1.25. Does he have enough money?

7. Carla wants to buy a notebook for $0.55, a pen for $0.90, and a ruler for $0.85. She has $2.50. Is this enough money?

yes

134

Connecting Fractions to Decimals

Write a fraction or a mixed number and a decimal for each.

1.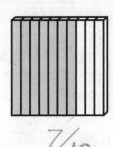

7/10

_____

2.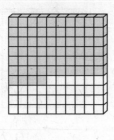

_____

3.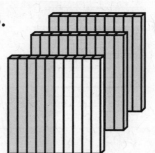

_____

4.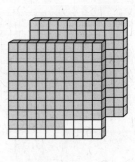

_____

Write the decimal. You may use a calculator to help you.

5. $12\frac{3}{10}$ __12,3__

6. $18\frac{70}{100}$ __18,7__

7. $\frac{02}{100}$ __.02__

8. $6\frac{9}{10}$ __6.9__

9. sixteen and two tenths __16.2__

10. eight and six tenths __8.6__

11. ten and ninety-nine hundredths _____

MIXED APPLICATIONS

12. Ila spent $0.65 of her $1.00 allowance. Write a fraction to show what part of the dollar she spent.

_____

13. A decimal number has a 2 in the tens place, a 6 in the ones place, and a 7 in the hundredths place. Write the number.

_____

VISUAL THINKING

A number line can show decimals and fractions. Find each letter on the number line. Then write a mixed number for the decimal or a decimal for the mixed number.

3	A	$3\frac{2}{10}$	$3\frac{3}{10}$	$3\frac{4}{10}$	C	$3\frac{6}{10}$	$3\frac{7}{10}$	$3\frac{8}{10}$	E	4
3.0	3.1	3.2	B	3.4	3.5	3.6	D	3.8	3.9	4.0

$\frac{3}{1000} = .00$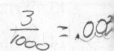

14. A _____

15. B _____

16. C _____

17. D _____

18. E _____

Unit 12

Core Skills Math, Grade 4

Name _____   Date _____

Decimals: Comparing and Ordering

Compare. Write <, >, or =.

1.
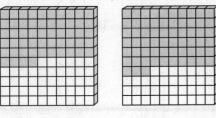

0.54 ◯ 0.63

2.
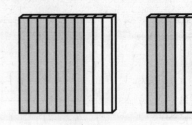

0.7 ◯ 0.3

3. 0.8 ◯ 0.2   **4.** 2.26 ◯ 2.29   **5.** 32.54 ◯ 32.41

6. 0.18 ◯ 0.25   **7.** 96.30 ◯ 96.3   **8.** 27.18 ◯ 27.81

Order the decimals from greatest to least.

9. 3.5, 0.46, 5.8, 5.62 _____

10. 52.43, 51.75, 51.7, 52.41 _____

MIXED APPLICATIONS

Use the table for Exercises 11 and 12.

11. Which student threw the softball the greatest distance? The shortest distance?

_____

12. Who threw the softball farther, LeRoy or Joseph?

_____

Kent School – Softball Throw	
Student	**Distance Thrown (in m)**
Carmen	18.08
Beatrice	22.95
LeRoy	20.5
Joseph	22.36
Irene	18.8

NUMBER SENSE

Use the digits 4, 5, 6, and 7 once in each number.

13. Write the largest decimal number possible. _____ _____ . _____ _____

14. Write the smallest decimal number possible. _____ _____ . _____ _____

Unit 12
Core Skills Math, Grade 4

Equivalent Fractions and Decimals

Write the number as hundredths in fraction form and decimal form.

1. $\frac{5}{10}$ Think: 5 tenths is how many hundredths?

_____

2. $\frac{9}{10}$ 3. 0.2   4. 0.8

_____   _____   _____

Write the number as tenths in fraction form and decimal form.

5. $\frac{40}{100}$ 6. $\frac{10}{100}$ 7. 0.60

_____   _____   _____

8. Billy walks $\frac{6}{10}$ mile to school each day. Write $\frac{6}{10}$ as hundredths in fraction form and in decimal form.

_____

9. Four states have names that begin with the letter A. This represents 0.08 of all the states. Write 0.08 as a fraction.

_____

Add Fractional Parts of 10 and 100

Find the sum.

1. $\frac{2}{10} + \frac{43}{100}$

Think: Write $\frac{2}{10}$ as a fraction with a denominator of 100.

_____

2. $\frac{17}{100} + \frac{6}{10}$

3. $\frac{9}{100} + \frac{4}{10}$

4. $\frac{7}{10} + \frac{23}{100}$

_____   _____   _____

5. $0.48 + 0.30$

6. $0.25 + 0.34$

7. $0.66 + 0.06$

_____   _____   _____

8. Ned's frog jumped $\frac{38}{100}$ meter. Then his frog jumped $\frac{4}{10}$ meter. How far did Ned's frog jump in all?

9. Keiko walks $\frac{5}{10}$ kilometer from school to the park. Then she walks $\frac{19}{100}$ kilometer from the park to her home. How far does Keiko walk in all?

_____

_____

Identify and Extend a Pattern

When you look at a shape pattern, think about the shape and position of the figures. Determine when the pattern begins to repeat.

Circle the pattern. Then draw the shape that continues the pattern.

1.  _____

2.  _____

3.  _____

4.  _____

5. 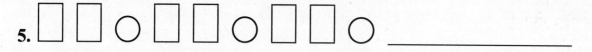 _____

6.  _____

VISUAL THINKING

Draw the shape that continues the pattern.

7.

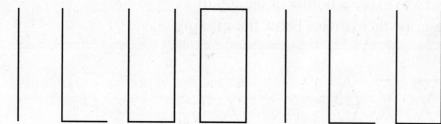 _____

Name _____ Date _____

Describe and Draw Shape Patterns

Solve each problem.

1. Marta is using this pattern to decorate a picture frame.
   Describe the pattern. Draw the next three figures in
   the pattern.

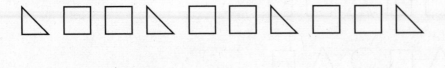

   _____

   _____

2. Describe the pattern. Draw the next three figures in
   the pattern. How many circles are in the sixth figure
   in the pattern?

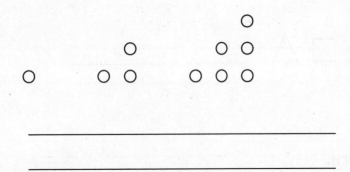

   _____

3. Larry stencils this pattern to make a border at the top of
   his bedroom walls. Describe the pattern. Draw the missing
   figure in the pattern

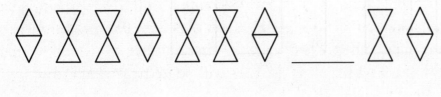

   _____

   _____

Number Patterns

Use the rule to write the first twelve numbers in the pattern.
Describe another pattern in the numbers.

1. Rule: Add 8.   First term: 5

Think: Add 8

5

_____

_____

2. Rule: Subtract 7.   First term: 95

_____

_____

3. Rule: Alternate adding 15 and subtracting 10.   First term: 4

_____

_____

4. Rule: Alternate adding 1 and multiplying by 2.   First term: 2

_____

_____

5. Barb is making a bead necklace. She strings 1 white bead, then 3 blue beads, then 1 white bead, and then repeats the pattern. Write the numbers for the first eight beads that are white. What is a rule for the pattern?

_____

6. An artist is arranging tiles in rows to decorate a wall. Each new row has 2 fewer tiles than the row below it. If the first row has 23 tiles, how many tiles will be in the seventh row?

_____

Problem Solving

FIND A PATTERN

1. Diego's exercise schedule follows a pattern. He exercises for 5 minutes on Monday, 8 minutes on Tuesday, 11 minutes on Wednesday, and 14 minutes on Thursday. For how many minutes does Diego exercise on Friday?

_____

on Saturday?

_____

2. Megan is saving money for new running shorts. She saves 1 penny the first day. On the second day she saves 2 pennies, on the third day she saves 4 pennies, and on the fourth day she saves 8 pennies. How many pennies will she save on the fifth day?

_____

on the sixth day?

_____

MIXED APPLICATIONS

> **STRATEGIES**
> • Guess and Check • Find a Pattern
> • Write a Number Sentence • Draw a Picture

Choose a strategy and solve.

3. It is 4:00 when Ned and Sue begin a math project. Ned finishes it in 15 minutes. Sue finishes 8 minutes later than Ned. At what time does Sue finish the math project?

_____

4. Zack and Bob play a pattern game. Zack says 4, and Bob says 8. Zack says 5, and Bob says 10. Zack says 6, and Bob says 12. What does Bob say when Zack says 7? When Zack says 9?

_____

VISUAL THINKING

5. Draw the next two shapes in the pattern.

 _____ _____

Problem Solving

FIND A SHAPE OR NUMBER PATTERN

In some patterns, a shape is repeated but its size or position changes. Draw the next four figures in each pattern.

1.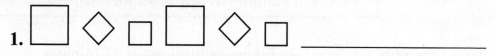

2.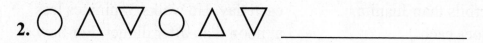

3.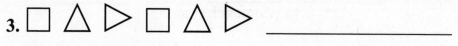

4.

Eric has a puzzle for his classmates. When he says 25, the answer is 125. When he says 56, the answer is 156. When he says 82, the answer is 182.

5. What is the pattern?

_____

6. If the answer is 198, what did Eric say?

_____

7. Eric changes the rule to his pattern. When he says 25, the answer is 45. The new pattern has only one rule. What is the rule?

_____

8. If the rule is Add 15 and Eric says 30, what are the next three numbers in the pattern?

_____

MIXED REVIEW

Write each number in expanded form.

9. 856 _____

10. 4,315 _____

Write the number that is 10,000 more.

11. 56,702 _____

12. 174,913 _____

Problem Solving

CHOOSE A STRATEGY

Choose a strategy and solve.

> **STRATEGIES**
> • Act It Out • Guess and Check • Make a Model
> • Draw a Picture • Write a Number Sentence

1. Cathy and Juanita have 14 gerbils. Cathy has 2 more gerbils than Juanita. How many gerbils does each girl have?

_____

_____

2. Ed walks his dog for 15 minutes each day. He walks 3 minutes less at noon than after dinner. For how many minutes does Ed walk his dog each time?

_____

_____

3. Hank spent $16 at the book sale. He spent $2 less on the fish book than he spent on the bird book. How much did he spend on each item?

_____

_____

4. Marta has a total of 17 goldfish in her tank. She has 5 more lionhead fish than fantail fish. How many of each kind of goldfish does Marta have?

_____

_____

5. Four children are standing in line. Matt is behind Pedro and in front of Bill. Jewel is in front of Pedro. Who is first in line? Who is last?

_____

_____

6. Dan has 15 animals on his farm. He has 5 cows and 3 goats. The rest are chickens. How many chickens does Dan have?

_____

_____

NUMBER SENSE

7. Look at Exercises 1 and 2. What can you do if you guess and are not correct?

_____

_____

_____

144

Name _____   Date _____

Problem-Solving Strategy

WORK BACKWARD

Solve. Make a flowchart and work backward.

1. Elena bought a belt for $12 and a scarf for $6. Later her mother gave her $10. Then Elena had $15. How much money did she have before she bought the belt and scarf?

   _____

2. Dan picked a number and added 8. Next, he multiplied by 4. Then he subtracted 5. The result was 35. What number did Dan pick?

   _____

MIXED APPLICATIONS

Choose a strategy and solve.

STRATEGIES
• Write a Number Sentence
• Work Backward • Draw a Picture

3. Peter rides his bike 3 kilometers each day. How many kilometers does he ride in 30 days?

   _____

4. Eric is 2 inches shorter than Peter and 3 inches taller than Julie. Jill is 1 inch shorter than Julie. Who is the tallest?

   _____

5. Myrta rode his bike after dinner. He watched television before dinner. He did his homework after he rode his bike. What was the second thing Myrta did?

MIXED REVIEW

Write the time in words and as shown on a digital clock.

6.

7.

8.

_____   _____   _____

_____   _____   _____

Problem-Solving Strategy

GUESS AND CHECK

Guess the answer. Then check it.

1. There are 25 plants in Tamara's garden. There are 4 times as many tomato plants as bean plants. How many tomato and bean plants are there?

   _____

   _____

2. José worked on a jigsaw puzzle for 6 hours. He worked 2 more hours in the afternoon than after dinner. How long did he work in the afternoon and after dinner?

   _____

   _____

MIXED APPLICATIONS

Choose a strategy and solve.

STRATEGIES
• Make a Table • Find a Pattern
• Work Backward • Write a Number Sentence

3. Michael paid $42.99 for a jacket on sale. The regular price of the jacket was $50.00. How much money did Michael save?

   _____

   _____

4. Tisha bought 2 books. Each book cost $6. Then she spent $10 for a CD. If Tisha has $4 left, how much did she start with?

   _____

   _____

5. Les bought a set of three shells for $25.00 and a frame to display the shells for $18.95. How much did he pay for these items?

   _____

6. Jerry bought a $15 game and a $6 book. Then his dad gave him $20. Now Jerry has $31. How much money did he have before he bought the game and book?

   _____

NUMBER SENSE

Find the missing factor.

7. $80 \times \rule{2cm}{0.4pt} = 5{,}600$ 8. $9 \times \rule{2cm}{0.4pt} = 72{,}000$ 9. $600 \times \rule{2cm}{0.4pt} = 6{,}000$

10. $6 \times \rule{2cm}{0.4pt} = 42{,}000$ 11. $500 \times \rule{2cm}{0.4pt} = 10{,}000$ 12. $40 \times \rule{2cm}{0.4pt} = 32{,}000$

13. $100 \times \rule{2cm}{0.4pt} = 7{,}500$ 14. $30 \times \rule{2cm}{0.4pt} = 9{,}000$ 15. $7 \times \rule{2cm}{0.4pt} = 49{,}000$

Problem Solving

MULTISTEP PROBLEMS

Solve. You will need to use more than one step.

1. The gas tank in the school bus holds 32 gallons of gas. On Monday, 8 gallons were used. From Tuesday to Wednesday, 16 more gallons were used. How much gas is left in the tank?

    _____

2. Martha left school at 3:15. She spent 15 minutes on safety patrol duty. It took her 20 minutes to get home. How many minutes are there until her tap dance class starts at 4:30?

    _____

3. Mr. Woo is driving 1,353 miles from Memphis to Boston. He drove 324 miles the first day and 372 miles the second day. How many miles are left to drive?

    _____

4. Miami gets about 5 feet of rain each year. Atlanta gets about 4 feet. What is the combined rainfall total each year for the two cities in inches?

    _____

MIXED APPLICATIONS

Choose a strategy and solve.

STRATEGIES
• Draw a Picture • Guess and Check
• Work Backward

5. Ray spent $3 on a magazine. He spent half of his remaining money on a poster. Then he spent $2 on a snack. Now Ray has $12. How much money did Ray have to begin with?

    _____

6. A sparkle flashlight costs 15¢ more than a plain flashlight. The total cost for both flashlights is 99¢. What is the cost of each flashlight?

    _____

WRITER'S CORNER

7. Write a problem that requires more than one step to solve.

    _____

    _____

147

Problem Solving

CHOOSE THE METHOD

Choose which method you would use to solve the problem: calculator, mental math, draw a model, or pencil and paper. Then solve.

1. Mr. Wade collects $900 from the sales of a $3 magazine at his newsstand. How many issues does he sell?

_____

2. Mr. Wade sells 85 copies of a magazine that costs $1.25. How much money does he collect from the sales of this magazine?

_____

MIXED APPLICATIONS

Choose a method and solve.

3. Mr. Wade carries 15 different newspapers. He carries 5 more than 4 times as many magazines. How many different magazines does he carry?

_____

4. Mr. Wade sells about 480 newspapers a day. Does he sell more than 4,000 papers in one week?

_____

5. Mr. Wade can place five types of magazines on a shelf. News magazines are in the middle of one shelf. Business and cooking magazines are at each end of the same shelf. Sports magazines are between news and cooking magazines. Where are the nature magazines?

_____

6. Mr. Wade opens his newsstand and works for 5 hours. Then he takes a 1-hour break. After the break, he works for 6 hours and 15 minutes until closing time at 6:10 P.M. What time did Mr. Wade open his newsstand?

_____

VISUAL THINKING

7. Write a problem that could be solved using the picture.

_____

_____

Problem Solving

MORE MULTISTEP PROBLEMS

Solve. You will need to use more than one step.

1. Raya rides 8 miles from her home to Spanish class. If she travels to class and back once a week, how far does she ride in 4 weeks?

2. Raya rents a Learning Spanish DVD for 4 days. The first day costs $2.75 and each additional day costs $1.50. What is the total cost for the 4-day rental?

3. Raya plans a 6-day trip to Mexico with her Spanish class. The cost is $65 per day for the hotel and food, and $279 for airfare. What is the total cost of the trip?

4. Raya takes a lot of photos. She takes 285 photos using her digital camera. She also uses 4 rolls of 24-photo film in her film camera. How many photos is this?

MIXED APPLICATIONS

5. Raya's class took a tour of a Mexican museum at 10:30 A.M. and left 5 hours 15 minutes later. At what time did they leave?

6. A large woven wall hanging in the museum is 16 feet wide and 50 feet tall. What is the area of the wall hanging?

SOCIAL STUDIES CONNECTION

The unit of currency (money) in Mexico is the *peso*. One month one U.S. dollar ($1) was equal to about 9 pesos.

Raya gave each storekeeper 100 pesos. How many pesos did she receive in change for each purchase?

7.

8.

9.

149

Name _____ Date _____

Problem Solving

FIND THE HIDDEN QUESTION

A *hidden question* is a question you must answer before you can solve a problem.
Find the hidden question. Then solve.

1. George works 4 hours a day at Sound Station. He can unpack a carton in 20 minutes. George has 3 cartons to unpack today. How much time does George have to do other work?

2. George orders music DVDs from recording companies. This week he places orders totaling $98 and $47. How much money is left in his weekly budget of $250?

3. George records two 16-minute programs and one 27-minute program on a 2-hour tape. How much recording time is left on the tape?

4. One MP3 player costs $284. George has saved $156. He then adds $32 from his paycheck. How much more does he need to save?

MIXED APPLICATIONS

STRATEGIES
• Find the Hidden Question • Work Backward
• Guess and Check • Draw a Picture

Choose a strategy and solve.

5. DVDs come in packs of 12 and 16. Tanya ordered 5 packs and received 76 tapes. How many packs of each size did she order?

6. Paula buys two 90-minute tapes for $2.49 each and one 60-minute tape. She pays $6.97. How much does the 60-minute tape cost?

MIXED REVIEW

Estimate the quotient or product.

7. $63 \times 13 =$ _____

8. $21 \times 12 =$ _____

9. $59 \times 22 =$ _____

10. $88 \times 41 =$ _____

11. $4\overline{)3,175}$ 12. $6\overline{)5,500}$ 13. $8\overline{)4,725}$ 14. $7\overline{)5,000}$ 15. $9\overline{)7,327}$

150

© Houghton Mifflin Harcourt Publishing Company

Unit 13
Core Skills Math, Grade 4

Problem-Solving Strategy

WRITE A NUMBER SENTENCE

Write a number sentence and solve.

1. The Handy Hardware store sold 40 feet of plastic pipe one week, 10 feet less the second week, and 72 feet the third week. How much pipe was sold in the three weeks?

   _____

   _____

2. Mr. Chen buys 2 trash cans for $16 each and a saw for $10. He returns a brush he bought last week for a credit of $7. How much is Mr. Chen's bill?

   _____

   _____

MIXED APPLICATIONS

Choose a strategy and solve.

STRATEGIES
• Make a Table • Write a Number Sentence • Draw a Picture

3. In July, the hardware store sold 23 bags of fertilizer and 16 bags of mulch. In August, the store sold 27 bags of fertilizer and 14 bags of mulch. Were more bags of fertilizer and mulch sold in July or August?

   _____

4. There were 63 nails left in one box, 29 in another box, and 44 in a third box. Estimate the total number of nails.

   _____

5. Mrs. Gonzalez buys a screwdriver for $5 and a pair of pliers for $6. She gives Mr. Miller a $20 bill. How much change does she receive?

   _____

6. Mr. Miller rearranges some paint on the shelves. White is on the right end. Red is not next to blue. Green is next to white. Yellow is not at the other end. Blue is between two other colors. Write the colors displayed from left to right.

   _____

WRITER'S CORNER

7. Write a problem that can be solved using a number sentence.

   _____

   _____

Problem Solving

MAKING DECISIONS

Lu wants to play in a string instrument group. She will need her own violin for at least 18 months. Lu considers these three options.

> Option 1: Rent a violin. Pay $40 a month.
> Option 2: Buy a violin. Pay $250 down and $35 a month for 9 months.
> Option 3: Buy a violin. Pay $33 a month for 18 months.

1. How much will the violin cost using Option 2?

_____

2. For 18 months, what is the most expensive option?

_____

3. For 18 months, what is the least expensive option?

_____

4. Lu will pay the least amount per month with which option?

_____

5. What is a reason for Lu to choose Option 2?

_____

6. What is a reason for Lu to choose Option 3?

_____

MIXED APPLICATIONS

Choose a strategy and solve.

> ### STRATEGIES
> • Draw a Picture • Guess and Check
> • Act It Out • Find a Pattern

7. There are 6 packages of rolls in the refrigerator. There are 8 rolls in each package. How many rolls are there in all?

_____

8. Two boxes weigh a total of 78 pounds. One box is 22 pounds heavier than the other box. How much does each box weigh?

_____

WRITER'S CORNER

9. Use the payment options for Exercises 1–6. Write a paragraph telling which option you would choose.

_____

_____

Interpret the Remainder

In word problems, you need to know what to do with any remainder.

- The remainder may tell you to round the answer up.
- The remainder may be dropped. • The remainder may be a part of the answer.
- The remainder may be the answer.

Solve. Tell what you did with the remainder.

1. Mr. Topaz is planting tomato plants. He wants to put exactly 15 plants in each row. He has 137 plants. How many full rows can he plant?

_____

2. Marian has 106 photos to put in a new album. Each page holds 16 photos. How many photos will be on the last page she uses?

_____

3. Ms. Plummer needs to cover 235 square feet of land with gravel. Each bag of gravel will cover 32 square feet. How many bags of gravel will she need?

_____

4. Neal brought 9 oranges to the park. He shared them equally among himself and 3 friends. How many oranges did each person get?

_____

MIXED APPLICATIONS	STRATEGIES
	• Use Estimation • Draw a Picture
	• Guess and Check • Write a Number Sentence

5. Penny spends $5.20 on bus fare for 4 round trips. What is the cost of a one-way bus fare?

_____

6. On Sunday, 83 tourists will travel to a museum in minibuses. Each minibus can hold 6 passengers. How many minibuses are needed?

_____

WRITER'S CORNER

7. Write a division problem that has a remainder. Solve the problem and tell what to do with the remainder.

_____

_____

Answer Key

Page 1

1. 10,607; ten thousand, six hundred seven
2. 90,500; 90,000 + 500
3. 30,000 + 4,000 + 60; thirty-four thousand, sixty
4. 7,864; seven thousand, eight hundred sixty-four
5. two thousand, three hundred forty-eight
6. 3,915
7. 702 tens; longs
8. 111 hundreds; flats
9. 21 tens, 21 ones; longs and units
10. 12 thousands, 12 tens, 12 ones; cubes, longs, and units

Page 2

1. 87
2. 432
3. 905
4. 4,707
5. 6,024
6. 7,145
7. 2,001
8. $1,427
9. Sue
10. $3,045
11. c.

Page 3

1. 400; 4 hundreds
2. 40,000; 4 ten thousands
3. 40; 4 tens
4. 400,000; 4 hundred thousands
5. 30,000; 3 ten thousands
6. 0; 0 tens
7. 8,000; 8 thousands
8. 900,000; 9 hundred thousands
9. 814,206; 800,000 + 10,000 + 4,000 + 200 + 6
10. 4 zeros; 40,000
11. 289,300; 200,000 + 80,000 + 9,000 + 300
12. a. subtract 40,000
    b. add 20

Page 4

1. thousands
2. millions
3. ones
4. 68,016,018
5. 640,540,086
6. 13,579,410
7. 835,270,100
8. false
9. true
10. false
11. true
12. a. 8
    b. 1

Page 5

1. 100,000 + 2,000 + 60; one hundred two thousand, sixty
2. 563,400; 500,000 + 60,000 + 3,000 + 400
3. 380,962; three hundred eighty thousand, nine hundred sixty-two
4. 400; 4 hundreds
5. 500,000; 5 hundred thousands
6. one hundred forty-five thousand, nine hundred eighty-seven dollars
7. $10.00
8. 1,290.00
9. seven hundred forty-five and ten cents

Page 6

1. 90,000,000; 9 ten millions
2. 900,000,000; 9 hundred millions
3. one hundred million, seventy thousand; 100,000,000 + 70,000
4. 200,504,908; two hundred million, five hundred four thousand, nine hundred eight
5. 70,084,039; 70,000,000 + 80,000 + 4,000 + 30 + 9

Possible answers are given for 6–7.

6. 1,150,000; one million, one hundred fifty thousand; 1,000,000 + 100,000 + 50,000
7. 739,000; seven hundred thirty-nine thousand; 700,000 + 30,000 + 9,000
8. one thousand, six hundred nine or sixteen hundred nine
9. 1,000 + 800 + 30

Page 7

1. 30
2. 700
3. 7
4. 9,000
5. 30,000
6. 500
7. 800,000
8. 6,000
9. 6,300; 10; 530
10. 2,783; 10; 7,283
11. 47,163; 10; 34,258
12. 26,475; 10; 503,497
13. 9,000
14. Ravens vs. Panthers

Page 8

1. 76,000
2. 8,050
3. 240,000
4. 72
5. 4,700
6. 256
7. 204,000
8. 3,200 tickets
9. 243 bags

Page 9

1. >
2. >
3. >
4. >
5. <
6. =
7. 2,345; 12,123; 22,486
8. 23,676; 32,076; 32,570
9. 68,921; 69,129; 70,291
10. 99,099; 99,900; 99,909
11. Map A
12. 147,046 sq mi
13. 31,700; 23,000; 22,300; 9,910; 7,550

Page 10

1. >
2. <
3. >
4. <
5. >
6. <
7. 52 < 56
8. 67 < 76
9. 1,239 < 1,339
10. 84 > 48
11. 2,094 > 2,049
12. 26,847 > 26,784
13. 2,875 m
14. 924 m
15. Mount McKinley
16. Mount Rushmore
17. Mount Rainier

Page 11

1. <
2. >
3. <
4. =
5. 2,345; 2,347; 2,435
6. 2,345,567; 2,345,657; 2,435,657
7. Oklahoma, Kentucky, Alabama
8. four hundred ninety-three thousand, seven hundred eighty-two; 400,000 + 90,000 + 3,000 + 700 + 80 + 2
9. Answers will vary but should mention that most of Wyoming is undeveloped while the District of Columbia is the seat of the Federal Government.

Page 12

1. 60
2. 80
3. 50
4. 40
5. 60
6. 80
7. 50
8. 100
9. 500
10. 700
11. 900
12. 400
13. 800
14. 500
15. 300
16. 200

17. 3,000
18. 5,000
19. 6,000
20. 4,000
21. 9,000
22. 7,000
23. 44,000
24. 4,000
25. Possible answer: Since 100 is less than 1,000, rounding to the nearest hundred is usually closer to the actual number. Nearest hundred: 12,700; nearest thousand: 13,000; 12,700 is 16 more than 12,684 while 13,000 is 316 more.

Page 13

1. 30
2. 240
3. 450
4. 900
5. 1,800
6. 45,800
7. 3,000
8. 24,000
9. 125,000
10. 50,000
11. 120,000
12. 580,000
13. 100,000
14. 1,500,000
15. 2,400,000
16. 57,000,000
17. 156,000,000
18. 13,800 ft
19. Arctic Ocean
20. 2,350; 2,000
21. 125,680; 126,000
22. 1,234,500; 1,234,000

Page 14

1. 50
2. $3.80
3. 70
4. $2.50
5. 90
6. $1.30
7. 560
8. 230
9. 500
10. 200
11. $8.00
12. 200
13. 7,000

14. 2,000
15. 3,000
16. 1,000
17. 4,200 mi
18. 375 mi; 384 mi
19. 496 mi
20. 2,194 mi
21. 1,459 mi

Page 15

1. 1 row of 11, 11 rows of 1; 1, 11; 11, 1; 2
2. 1 row of 12, 12 rows of 1, 3 rows of 4, 4 rows of 3, 2 rows of 6, 6 rows of 2; 1, 12; 12, 1; 3, 4; 4, 3; 2, 6; 6, 2; 6
3. 1 row of 13, 13 rows of 1; 1, 13; 13, 1; 2
4. 1 row of 14, 14 rows of 1, 2 rows of 7, 7 rows of 2; 1, 14; 14, 1; 2, 7; 7, 2; 4
5. prime
6. composite
7. prime
8. composite
9. prime, 2
10. composite, 4

Page 16

1. 1, 2, 3, 6
2. 1, 5, 7, 35
3. 1, 19
4. 1, 3, 13, 39
5. 1, 2, 4, 11, 22, 44
6. 1, 2, 4, 8, 16, 32, 64
7. 1, 2, 4, 7, 8, 14, 28, 56
8. 1, 2, 4, 5, 8, 10, 16, 20, 40, 80
9. composite
10. prime
11. prime
12. composite
13. prime
14. composite
15. prime
16. composite
17. 1 row of 30; 2 rows of 15; 3 rows of 10; 5 rows of 6; 6 rows of 5; 10 rows of 3; 15 rows of 2; 30 rows of 1
18. 2, 3, 4, 6, 8, or 12 people
19. Check work.

Page 17

1. 59
2. Circle second column; 81
3. Circle second column; 65
4. Circle second column; 96
5. Circle both columns; 150
6. Circle both columns; 146
7. Circle first column; 128
8. Circle second column; 54
9. Circle second column; 78
10. Circle both columns; 174
11. Circle second column; 60
12. Circle first column; 175
13. Circle both columns; 140
14. 54
15. 98
16. Circle first column; 129
17. Circle both columns; 146
18. 57
19. 163
20. 135
21. 135
22. 133
23. 116
24. 125
25. 143
26. 178
27. 146
28. 161
29. Blue
30. White
31. 7, 4
32. 8, 9
33. 4, 1, 5

Page 18

1. Circle last column; 584
2. Circle middle column; 935
3. Circle first and last columns; 1,281
4. Circle first and last columns; 1,280
5. 386
6. Circle first and middle columns; 1,259
7. Circle middle column; 847
8. Circle first and middle columns; 1,125
9. Circle first and middle columns; 1,589
10. 957
11. 797
12. Circle last column; 881
13. Circle first and middle columns; 1,246

14. Circle all columns; 1,043
15. Circle middle column; 618
16. Circle last column; $473
17. Circle middle and last columns; $611
18. $384
19. Circle first and middle columns; $1,125
20. Circle first column; $1,177
21. $1,125
22. 661 pieces
23. 60
24. 80
25. 80
26. 40
27. $130
28. $60
29. $150
30. $20
31. 600
32. 400
33. 600
34. 900
35. $500
36. $600
37. $800
38. $800

Page 19

1. 89
2. 135
3. 1,930
4. 10,305
5. 2,806
6. 126
7. 757
8. $1,120
9. $5,758
10. $790
11. 133 min
12. $310
13. 5,239 cars; 5,295 cars; 11,266 cars
14. To find the least sum, the ones digits should be 5 and 9, the tens digits 3 and 4, and the hundreds digits 1 and 2.
Example: 135 + 249 = 384.
15. To find the greatest sum, the ones digits should be 1 and 2, the tens digits 3 and 4, and the hundreds digits 5 and 9.
Example: 942 + 531 = 1,473.

Page 20

Estimates may vary. One possible estimate is given.

1. 600
2. 610
3. 6,000; 6,023
4. 8,000; 8,121
5. 40,000; 37,901
6. 60,000; 58,621
7. 2,400
8. 5,000
9. 4,000
10. 4,089
11. 2,100
12. 2,134
13. 30,000
14. 33,884
15. 10,000
16. 10,060
17. 357 ft
18. 1,000 + 700 + 60
19. Yes. 176 + 152 = 328, and 328 > 325.

Page 21

1. 54
2. Circle; 37
3. 11
4. Circle; 17
5. Circle; 4
6. 31
7. Circle; 51
8. Circle; 49
9. Circle; 39
10. 10
11. 42
12. Circle; 35
13. Circle; 2
14. 24
15. Circle; 45
16. Circle; 19
17. 32
18. 20
19. 8
20. 18
21. 26
22. 8
23. 56
24. 25
25. 13
26. 19
27. 51
28. 67 garden hoses

29. 46 shovels
30. $8 + 9 = 17; 17 - 8 = 9$
31. $9 + 2 = 11; 11 - 9 = 2$
32. $3 + 8 = 11; 8 + 3 = 11$
33. $11 - 6 = 5; 11 - 5 = 6$

Page 22

1. 225
2. 495
3. 604
4. 119
5. 391
6. $680
7. $408
8. $568
9. $554
10. $59
11. 549
12. 824
13. $76
14. $294
15. 139 kg
16. 1,433 kg
17. b.

Page 23

Estimates may vary for 1–8. One possible estimate is given.

1. 3,000
2. 30,000; 32,384
3. 30,000; 21,109
4. 10,000
5. 30,000; 30,981
6. 5,000
7. 61,000; 60,650
8. 30,000; 29,135
9. 900 seats
10. 4,222 fans
11. 16,726; 12,739; 12,312; 12,120
12. 24,432 yd
13. 890,000
14. 10,014,600

Page 24

Check regrouping for 1–4.

1. 77
2. 622
3. 496
4. 863
5. 531
6. 55
7. 11
8. 2,136
9. 5,111

10. 3,994
11. 9,104
12. 17,985
13. 315 stamps
14. 45 stamps
15. Check regrouping; 5,891
16. Possible explanation: In hundreds place you must subtract across the zero in thousands place. In tens place you do not need to subtract across a zero.

Page 25

1. 1,178
2. 678
3. 7,001
4. 646
5. 5,604
6. 8,316
7. 4,007
8. $11
9. $4
10. $17
11. a magazine and a comic book
12. Answer will vary.

Page 26

Estimates may vary. One possible estimate is given.

1. 3,000; 3,186
2. 8,000; 7,650
3. 4,000; 3,864
4. 8,000; 8,052
5. 2,000; 2,426
6. 5,000; 4,724
7. 6,000; 5,369
8. 3,000; 3,159
9. 11,000; 11,207
10. 10,000; 9,650
11. 2,000; 1,315
12. 1,000; 1,081
13. 12,000; 12,206
14. 10,000; 12,568
15. 319; 2,851; 2,902; 1,133
16. 7,205 kilowatt hr
17. >
18. <
19. =
20. 161
21. 584

Page 27

1. 1,086
2. 439
3. 9,430
4. 15,153
5. 3,975
6. 16,322
7. yes; $139 + 185 = 324$
8. about 600 mi
9. 9
10. 8
11. 7
12. 7,500
13. 1,800
14. 11,600
15. 1,700
16. 5,600
17. 7,000
18. 2,000
19. 12,000
20. 1,000
21. 6,000

Page 28

Check arrays for 1–3.

1. 12
2. 24
3. 14
4. 2
5. 8
6. 3
7. 16
8. 18
9. 24
10. 18
11. 10
12. 12
13. 27
14. 14
15. 4
16. 12
17. 6
18. 15
19. 6
20. 21
21. 9
22. 24
23. 15
24. 12
25. 18
26. 8
27. 21
28. 3

157

29. 16
30. 10 stamps
31. $15
32. 27 points
33. 27 points
34. 30 points

Page 29

Check arrays for 1–3.

4. 15
5. 25
6. 4
7. 10
8. 24
9. 30
10. 12
11. 35
12. 32
13. 16
14. 15
15. 20
16. 45
17. 8
18. 5
19. 20
20. 40
21. 36
22. 40
23. 15
24. 35
25. 45
26. 20
27. 28
28. 16
29. 32
30. 30 people
31. 12 helicopters
32. <
33. >
34. =
35. >
36. =
37. <

Page 30

Check arrays for 1–3.

1. 42
2. 28
3. 54
4. 42
5. 6
6. 7
7. 42
8. 14

9. 28
10. 18
11. 49
12. 36
13. 48
14. 56
15. 72
16. 14
17. 36
18. 21
19. 54
20. 30
21. 28 strings
22. 5 pianos
23. Middle circle factors, clockwise from 5: 1, 4, 6, 2, 0; Outer circle products, clockwise from 0: 54, 30, 18

Page 31

Check arrays for 1–3.

1. 32
2. 27
3. 64
4. 72
5. 24
6. 9
7. 56
8. 18
9. 8
10. 63
11. 32
12. 72
13. 64
14. 54
15. 16
16. 45
17. 48
18. 81
19. 27
20. 36
21. 40
22. 56 batches
23. 48 muffins
24. b., 14

Page 32

1. 24
2. 54
3. 32
4. 18
5. 56
6. 20

7. 0
8. 16
9. 72
10. 24
11. 35
12. 81
13. 28
14. 30
15. 63
16. 16
17. 0
18. 42
19. 64
20. 21
21. 48
22. 49
23. 6
24. 36
25. 0
26. 45
27. 24, 32, 40, 48, 56, 64, 72
28. 21, 28, 35, 42, 49, 56, 63
29. 64 ears of corn
30. 29 green peppers
31. 7,114
32. 2,809
33. 4,481
34. 5,909
35. 1,666

Page 33

1. 6, 3, 18
2. 63, 7, 9
3. 5, 4, 20
4. 48, 8, 6
5. $2 \times 8 = 16$
6. $42 = 6 \times 7$
7. $3 \times 5 = 15$
8. $36 = 9 \times 4$
9. $72 = 8 \times 9$
10. $5 \times 6 = 30$
11. 7 years old
12. 3 counselors

Page 34

Check models for 1–4.

1. $5 \times n = 40$; $5 \times 8 = 40$; $4 \times 8 = 32$ blue beads
2. $4 \times n = 24$; $4 \times 6 = 24$; $3 \times 6 = 18$ monkeys

3. $8 \times n = 56$; $8 \times 7 = 56$; $7 \times 7 = 49$ in.
4. $6 \times n = 18$; $6 \times 3 = 18$; $5 \times 3 = 15$ markers
5. 36 white cars
6. 25 more points

Page 35

Check drawings for 1–3.

1. 3
2. 6
3. 9
4. 9
5. 1
6. 6
7. 2
8. 4
9. 7
10. 7
11. 5
12. 8
13. 2
14. 9
15. 8
16. 2
17. 5
18. 8
19. 3
20. 5
21. 6
22. 4
23. 1
24. 8 cages
25. 8 days

Check drawings for 26–28.

26. 5 unit cubes
27. 9 unit cubes
28. 9 unit cubes

Page 36

Check drawings for 1–3.

1. 6
2. 5
3. 5
4. 8
5. 7
6. 3
7. 8
8. 7
9. 4
10. 9
11. 1
12. 5
13. 5

158

14. 3
15. 6
16. 9
17. 2
18. 5 bookshelves
19. $15
20. 5, 9
21. 3, 9
22. 8

Page 37

Check drawings for 1–3.

1. 5
2. 6
3. 3
4. 2
5. 7
6. 3
7. 9
8. 5
9. 9
10. 1
11. 6
12. 4
13. 4
14. 2
15. 7
16. 1
17. 8
18. $45
19. 4 trips
20. how many in each group; 4 tires
21. how many groups; 8 boxes

Page 38

Check drawings for 1–3.

1. 4
2. 5
3. 3
4. 7
5. 2
6. 3
7. 7
8. 4
9. 1
10. 5
11. 9
12. 6
13. 8
14. 6
15. 8
16. 1

17. 2
18. 9
19. 3
20. 3
21. 7
22. 2
23. 4
24. 7 roses
25. 54 flowers
26. $5 \times 9 = 45; 45 \div 9 = 5; 45 \div 5 = 9$
27. $48 \div 8 = 6; 6 \times 8 = 48; 8 \times 6 = 48$
28. $9 \times 8 = 72; 72 \div 9 = 8; 72 \div 8 = 9$

Page 39

1. $72 \div 9 = 8$; 8 pens
2. $7 \times 2 = 14$; 14 bags
3. $280 \div 7 = 40$ min per day, $40 \div 2$ sessions = 20; 20 min
4. 45 min
5. $4 \times 3 = 12$
6. $4 \times 2 = 8$
7. $4 \times 4 = 16$
8. $4 \times 8 = 32$

Page 40

1. months
2. minutes
3. minutes
4. second
5. a.
6. c.
7. about 4:00 P.M. (3:55)
8. less than 1 hr
9. Last two clocks: 3:00 and 8:00.

Page 41

1. 16 hr
2. 65 min, or 1 hr, 5 min
3. 35 min
4. 5 hr
5. 7:45 A.M.
6. 35 min
7. 7:10 A.M.
8. 10:15 A.M.; 11:00 A.M.; 11:45 A.M.; 12:30 P.M.; 1:15 P.M.

Page 42

1. 4:30
2. 6:45
3. Men's basketball
4. 6:30
5. 1 hr
6. 45 min
7. 6:50
8. 345 boys and girls
9. Answers will vary.

Page 43

1. Train B
2. Train A
3. one
4. 15 min
5. 11:00 A.M.
6. $7
7. 3 hr, 36 min, 14 seconds
8. 6 hr, 42 min, 5 seconds

Page 44

1. 9:15
2. 2:15
3. 11:30
4. 3
5. 2:45
6. Andy, Len, Debra, Matt
7. minutes
8. hours
9. minutes
10. minutes

Page 45

1. 48
2. 1,140
3. 21
4. 168
5. 730
6. 3
7. 9
8. 360; 21,600
9. 13
10. 8; 11,520
11. 17,520
12. 202
13. 604,800
14. 8, 18
15. 4
16. 5, 2
17. 20,160
18. 1,461 days
19. 540 hr

20. 2 hr
21. Answers will vary. Possible answers: Divide the number of days by 7 days per week; Multiply the number of years by 365 days per year, multiply the product by 24 hours per day, and then multiply that product by 60 minutes per hour.

Page 46

1. a.
2. c.
3. $0.29
4. yes
5. yes
6. $9.53
7. $7.74
8. $11.22
9. $5.51
10. $12.13
11. $1.64

Page 47

1. No
2. Yes
3. No
4. Yes
5. No
6. Yes
7. Yes
8. Yes. Possible explanation: $10 \times 4 = 40$. 5×4 is half this amount, or 20. $40 + 20 = 60$.
9. No. Possible explanation: $3.5 \times 200 = 700$, so 3.5×180 cannot be $> 1,000$.

Page 48

1. 4 pennies, 5 quarters
2. Answers will vary. Possible answers: 1 $5 bill, 3 quarters, 2 dimes; 5 $1 bills, 9 dimes, 1 nickel
3. $13.92
4. $3.16

5. 10 dimes
6. 6 quarters, 3 dimes
7. $1.35, $1.40, $1.50, $1.75, $2.00

Page 49

1. Answers will vary. Possible answers: puffy paint and any marker; glitter paint and a thin or medium marker.
2. Answers will vary. Possible answers: a vest or sweatshirt and any one paint or marker; a jacket, thin marker, and puffy paint.
3. $17.17
4. 21 paints
5. Answers will vary.

Page 50

1. 72; 80; 152
2. 24; 160; 184
3. 10; 100; 500; 610
4. 27; 90; 600; 717
5. 15; 450; 500; 965
6. $72
7. $264
8. 1 $10, 2 $5, 4 $1; 1 $10, 1 $5, 9 $1; 1 $10, 14 $1; 4 $5, 4 $1; 3 $5, 9 $1; 2 $5, 14 $1; 1 $5, 19 $1; 24 $1

Page 51

1. 574
2. 342
3. 951
4. 875
5. 672
6. 728
7. 770
8. 957
9. 680
10. 984
11. 812
12. 825
13. 880
14. 954
15. 772
16. 868
17. 675 offices
18. 412 offices
19. 642; $6 \times 7 = 42$; $6 \times 100 = 600$; $42 + 600 = 642$
20. 624; $3 \times 8 = 24$; $3 \times 200 = 600$; $24 + 600 = 624$
21. 820; $4 \times 5 = 20$; $4 \times 200 = 800$; $20 + 800 = 820$

Page 52

1. 1,968
2. 1,892
3. 1,953
4. 915
5. 3,625
6. 3,664
7. 2,425
8. 858
9. 8,460
10. 2,970
11. 1,602
12. 1,648
13. 6,944
14. 15 hr
15. $14
16. 468 people
17. 2,108 people
18. 3
19. 3
20. 7; 1; 0

Page 53

Estimates may vary for 1–9.
One possible estimate is given.
1. 4,000; 4,192
2. 8,000; 7,144
3. 12,000; 13,095
4. 28,000; 29,032
5. 49,000; 45,626
6. 28,000; 25,368
7. 30,000; 27,798
8. 21,000; 21,642
9. 24,000; 21,720
10. 23,750 copies
11. 3,258 newspapers
12. 1 hr 35 min
13. 177 customers
14. Answer will vary.

Page 54

Estimates will vary for 1–8.
One possible estimate is given.
1. 140
2. 160
3. 3,000; 3,185
4. 5,600; 5,808
5. 6,000; 6,351
6. 3,000; 3,228
7. 42,000; 38,612
8. 54,000; 52,461
9. 365
10. 2,718

11. 516
12. 16,424
13. 3,318
14. 27,810
15. 11,864
16. 2,142
17. 34,008
18. 5,925
19. 15,400 mi
20. 2 pilots
21. two thousand, three hundred forty-five; $2,000 + 300 + 40 + 5$
22. 40,096; $40,000 + 90 + 6$
23. 7,009
24. 14,059

Page 55

1. 5; 90; 900
2. 4; 140; 1,400
3. 1,560
4. 1,150
5. 300
6. 960
7. 2,460
8. 1,440
9. 2,160
10. 3,900
11. 5,360
12. 720 min
13. 1,440 min
14. 168 hr
15. 240 hr
16. 960 min
17. Questions will vary.

Page 56

Models may vary for 2–6.
1. 546
2. $(300 + 240 + 40 + 32)$; 612
3. $(400 + 120 + 40 + 12)$; 572
4. $(300 + 150 + 30 + 15)$; 495
5. $(400 + 180 + 60 + 27)$; 667
6. $(300 + 270 + 60 + 54)$; 684
7. No, he drew the model correctly, but when he multiplied 20×7 he wrote 14 instead of 140. His answer should be: $200 + 140 + 40 + 28 = 408$.
8. $6.10

Page 57

1. (54; 120; 540; 1,200); 1,914
2. (42; 480; 70; 800); 1,392
3. (6; 540; 40; 3,600); 4,186
4. $14 \times 24 = 336$ pages
5. $26 \times 19 = 494$ newspapers
6. 300
7. 4,000
8. 32,000
9. 2,800
10. 27,000
11. 7,200
12. 6; 150; 1,500
13. 8; 280; 2,800

Page 58

1. 1,824
2. 3,456
3. 1,428
4. 1,488
5. 1,896
6. 3,648
7. 897
8. 6,750
9. 1,827
10. 2,352
11. $n = 3,120$
12. $n = 2,394$
13. $n = 1,118$
14. $n = 3,128$
15. 2,184 hr
16. 756 mi
17. 384 mi
18. 648 mi
19. 720 mi
20. 616 mi

Page 59

1. a.
2. c.
3. c.
4. m (or dm)
5. m
6. km
7. cm
8. 5 dm
9. 10 m
10. 16 km
11. 2 m
12. 49 km
13. Fay (15 stickers)
14. a. 70 km, b. 52 km, c. 122 km

Page 60

1. b.
2. c.
3. b.
4. m
5. mm
6. cm
7. km
8. 23.2 cm
9. Jack's measurement of Kelly
10. 10,000
11. 100,000
12. 1,000,000

Page 61

1. in.
2. ft
3. yd
4. 3 yd
5. 16 ft
6. 23 mi
7. 400 yd
8. Mel
9. yardstick
10. Mississippi
11. 1,040 mi
12. Tennessee
13. in.
14. mi
15. ft

Page 62

1. L
2. mL
3. L
4. mL
5. 1 mL
6. 400 mL
7. 15 L
8. c.
9. b.
10. a.
11. the wide vase
12. 2 L
13. 350 mL
14. 20 mL
15. 250 mL
16. 4 L

Page 63

1. a.
2. b.
3. a.
4. b.
5. L
6. mL
7. L
8. L
9. mL
10. L
11. 4 scoops
12. 18 glasses
13. Problems will vary.

Page 64

1. qt or gal
2. c
3. gal
4. qt
5. tbsp
6. c or pt
7. 2 pt
8. 12 people

Answers will vary for 9–10.
Possible answers are given.

9. gallons, gallon, tablespoon
10. pt, qt, c

Page 65

1. g
2. g
3. kg
4. kg
5. g
6. kg
7. 1 g
8. 1,750 kg
9. 20 g
10. 450 kg
11. 3 kg
12. 725 g
13. Possible answer: Put the 5 kg and the 10 kg weights on one side of the scale and the 1 kg on the other side. Add oranges to the 1 kg side until the scale is balanced.

Page 66

1. kg
2. g
3. g
4. kg
5. a.

6. b.
7. 17 portions
8. 8 portions
9. 24 portions
10. 20 portions
11. 780 g
12. 7 trips
13. 780
14. 2,880
15. 660
16. 16,270
17. 1,495

Page 67

1. oz
2. lb
3. lb
4. T
5. lb
6. oz
7. 1 lb
8. 7 lb
9. 5 oz
10. 80
11. 26,000
12. 4
13. pounds
14. 4 lb, 8 oz
15. 3 lb

Page 68

1. b.
2. a.
3. b.
4. a.
5. a.
6. b.
7. 80
8. 0.002
9. 2,000
10. 35,000
11. 3 g
12. 0.02 L
13. 0.6 m
14. 0.15 g
15. 0.09 m
16. Suzanne
17. 92 g
18. 45.6 L
19. 91.2 L

Page 69

1. Gallons; Quarts
2. Years; Months
3. Pints; Cups
4. Weeks; Days
5. Answers will vary.
6. Answers will vary.
7. Answers will vary.

Page 70

1. 132; 128; 132
2. 38
3. 285
4. 270
5. 6,600
6. 13
7. 124
8. 15 gal 2 qt
9. 4 lb 11 oz
10. 12 hr 15 min
11. 35 min
12. 4 ft 10 in.
Answers will vary for 13–16.
One possible answer is given.
13. carton of milk
14. tube of toothpaste
15. container of liquid laundry detergent
16. package of cream cheese

Page 71

Check circling for 1–5.
1. 2
2. 1
3. 4
4. 5
5. 3
6. No
7. Yes
8. No
9. 2,314

Page 72

1. 5
2. 2
3. 3
4. 2
5. 4
6. 6
7. 400,000; 400; 40,000
8. 7; 3 pennies, 1 dime, 1 quarter, 2 $1 bills

Page 73

Check drawings for 1–5.
1. 3
2. 3
3. 5
4. 4
5. a.

Page 74

Answers for 1–6 tell the digit over which the first digit in the quotient should be placed.
1. 0
2. 8
3. 5
4. 8
5. 8
6. 7
7. 17
8. 13 r3
9. 13 r4
10. 24
11. 21 r3
12. 13
13. 29 r2
14. 11 r5
15. $8.34
16. 14 letters of each color
17. 4

Page 75

Answers for 1–5 tell the digit over which the first digit in the quotient should be placed.
1. 4
2. 7
3. 9
4. 6
5. 6
6. 84 r2
7. 65
8. 122 r5
9. 104 r3
10. about 81
11. about 189
12. about 97
13. records
14. 118 tapes per shelf
15. 2
16. 33
17. 114
18. 62

Page 76

Answers for 1–5 tell the digit over which the first digit in the quotient should be placed.
1. 1
2. 7
3. 6
4. 8
5. 6
Estimates may vary for 6–8. One possible estimate is given.
6. 103 r1; Estimate: 100
7. 202 r1; Estimate: 200
8. 107 r3; Estimate: 100
9. 100 r2
10. 100 r1
11. 200 r3
12. about 8 days
13. 199
14. 5 r2
15. 6 r1
16. 6 r3
Estimates may vary for 17–21. One possible estimate is given.
17. 8
18. 7
19. 5
20. 2
21. 7

Page 77

1. 318
2. 157 r3
3. 113 r2
4. 1,123 r1
5. 582
6. 1,509 r4
7. $197
8. Lees; Possible explanation: $632 ÷ 4 = $158; $328 ÷ 2 = $164; 158 < 164
9. 3
10. 63

Page 78

1. line segment
2. ray
3. point
4. line

Check drawings for 5–7.

8. no
9. yes
10. no
11. yes
12. a square
13. 11 lines
14. pentagon, star

Page 79

1. acute
2. right
3. obtuse
4. acute
5. right
6. obtuse
7. acute
8. 1 acute angle
9. 2 acute angles
10. 3 acute angles
11. 1 acute angle
12. 5,489
13. 75,618
14. 121,888
15. 5,872
16. 16,233
17. 60
18. 146 r3
19. 52 r1
20. 73 r3
21. 216
22. $4.30
23. $22.50

Page 80

Answers may vary for 1–4.
Possible answers are given.

1. parallel lines
2. perpendicular lines
3. intersecting lines
4. ray

Check drawings for 5–7.

8. 3:00 and 9:00
9. 1:50

Answers will vary for 10–12.
Accept reasonable definitions.

Page 81

1. b.
2. a.
3. b.
4. a.
5. line AB
6. lines AC and BD
7. perpendicular lines
8. Check work.

Page 82

1. acute
2. right
3. obtuse
4. Answers may vary.
   Possible answers:
   ∠MRO or ∠QRO
5. Answers may vary.
   Possible answers:
   ∠MRP or ∠QRN
6. Answers may vary.
   Possible answers:
   ∠MRN, ∠NRO,
   ∠PRO, ∠PRN,
   or ∠PRQ
7. acute
8. obtuse
9. 127 cm
10. 32 pages
11. 16¢
12. 18¢
13. 60¢

Page 83

Estimates may vary for 1–4.
Accept reasonable
measurements.

1. 50°
2. 110°
3. 90°
4. 70°

Check drawings for 5-10.

11. A, B, E; B, C, G; D, C, E, F

Page 84

Accept reasonable
measurements
for 1–3.

1. 70°
2. 20°
3. 110°

Check drawings for 4–6.
Accept reasonable angles.

7. 65°
8. west
9. Names may vary.
   Possible answers:
   ∠MRQ, ∠MRP,
   ∠MRO, ∠MRN,
   ∠NRO, ∠NRP, ∠NRQ,
   ∠ORP, ∠ORQ , ∠PRQ

Page 85

1. 50° + 75° = 125°
2. 140° + 20° = 160°
3. 30° + 90° + 45° =165°
4. 115°
5. 90°
6. 75°
7. 80°
8. 115° + 75° + 90° +
   80° = 360°
9. 50°; 60°; 70°
10. 50° + 60° + 70° =
    180°

Page 86

Check diagrams for 1–3.
Equations will vary. One
possible equation is given.

1. $x + 120° = 180°, x = 60°$
2. $225° − 130° = x,$
   $x = 95°$
3. $90° − 40° = x, x = 50°$

Page 87

1. angle
2. plane
3. line segment
4. point
5. Q, S, R
6. line segments
   QR, QS, SR
7. ray BA, ray BD, ray BC
8. Names may vary.
   Possible answers:
   ∠ABD, ∠ABC, ∠DBC
9. Check drawings.

10. Yes. A plane has 2
    dimensions and is flat.
    The sidewalk is
    described as flat, so it is
    a plane.
11. angle
12. line segment

Page 88

1. yes
2. yes
3. no
4. yes
5. yes
6. no

Check drawings for 7–9.

10. She should buy pencils
    in boxes.
11. $1.20; Explanations
    will vary but should
    reflect: 12 × $0.80 =
    $9.60; 2 × $4.20 =
    $8.40;
    $9.60 − 8.40 = $1.20

Page 89

1. 2 lines of symmetry
2. 3 lines of symmetry
3. 1 line of symmetry
4. 4 lines of symmetry
5. yes
6. no
7. yes
8. no

Check drawings for 9–12.

13. Answers will vary.
    Possible answer: eraser,
    chair, and window
14. 3,750 miles more
15. Check drawings for
    vertical symmetry.

Page 90

1. yes
2. yes
3. no

Check work for 4–6.

4. 2 lines of symmetry
5. 1 line of symmetry
6. 6 lines of symmetry

Check drawings for 7–9.

10. F, G, J, K, L
11. A, B, C, D, E, M
12. F; C; D

163

Page 91

1. yes
2. no
3. yes
4. no

Check work for 5–8.

5. 2 lines of symmetry
6. 2 lines of symmetry
7. 5 lines of symmetry
8. 5 lines of symmetry

Check drawings for 9–12.

13. Answers will vary. Possible answer: birdbath and garage door
14. Check drawing. Lines should be non-perpendicular lines of symmetry.
15. Check drawings.

Page 92

1. 24 in.
2. 32 m
3. 44 ft
4. 108 cm
5. 216 in.
6. 240 m
7. Check sketches. No. He needs 48 in.
8. 120 ft
9. 6 ft, 4 ft, 4 ft

Page 93

Check drawings for 1–3.

4. 25 square units; $5 \times 5 = 25$
5. 18 square units; $3 \times 6 = 18$
6. 12 square units
7. 10 square units
8. B and C
9. A and B; C and D
10. 270,000 sq km
11. 178,200 sq km

Page 94

1. 108 sq ft
2. 64 sq yd
3. 45 sq m
4. 78 sq in.
5. 150 sq cm
6. 56 sq ft
7. 96 sq ft
8. 420 pieces

Page 95

1. 40 sq m
2. 143 sq ft
3. 63 sq in.
4. 50 sq ft
5. 180 sq cm
6. 68 sq yd
7. 4 ft; 5 ft
8. 52 sq ft
9. 25 sq ft

Page 96

1. 7 ft
2. 12 m
3. 7 cm
4. 8 in.
5. 27 yd
6. 12 ft

Page 97

1. 2; 4; 0; quadrilateral, parallelogram, rhombus
2. quadrilateral, parallelogram, rectangle
3. quadrilateral, trapezoid
4. quadrilateral
5. quadrilateral, parallelogram, rhombus
6. quadrilateral, trapezoid
7. quadrilateral, parallelogram
8. a rhombus
9. a square or a rectangle

Page 98

1. scalene
2. isosceles
3. equilateral
4. isosceles
5. 31 hr
6. $310
7. about $1,320
8. $116.96
9. 4,200
10. 1,400
11. 1,100
12. 2,200

Page 99

1. right
2. acute
3. right
4. obtuse
5. Yes. An equilateral triangle has three acute angles so it is also an acute triangle.

6. $5.00
7. 380 empty spaces
8. pentagon
9. 2,000
10. 3,000
11. 56.49
12. 25.68
13. 3,589
14. 2,660
15. 28.63
16. 13.65
17. 6,842
18. 7,296

Page 100

1. 60°
2. 180°
3. 90°
4. acute
5. obtuse
6. acute
7. right
8. obtuse
9. acute
10. $\frac{1}{3}$ turn clockwise
11. 120°

Page 1

1. 8
2. 10
3. $\frac{3}{4}$
4. 2
5. 10
6. 3
7. 10
8. 12
9. 3
10. 9 cards
11. 9 sports cars
12. 60 stamps
13. 30 rocks
14. $3
15. $12
16. $8

Page 102

1. 2
2. $\frac{1}{3}$ of $12 = 4$
3. $\frac{1}{3}$ of $9 = 3$
4. $\frac{1}{5}$ of $5 = 1$
5. $\frac{1}{5}$ of $10 = 2$

164

6. $\frac{1}{5}$ of $15 = 3$

7. $2

8. 6 apples

9. 12; 4; 8; 3; 9

Page 103

1. $\frac{2}{6}$

2. $\frac{2}{4}$

3. $\frac{6}{8}$

4. $\frac{1}{3}$

5. Circle last figure.

6. Circle third figure.

Answers will vary for 7–10. Possible answers are given.

7. $\frac{2}{8}, \frac{3}{12}$

8. $\frac{2}{10}, \frac{3}{15}$

9. $\frac{4}{6}, \frac{6}{9}$

10. $\frac{6}{16}, \frac{9}{24}$

11. They each eat the same amount.

12. 3 eggs

Answers will vary for 13–14. Possible answers are given.

13. $\frac{12}{36}, \frac{6}{18}, \frac{3}{9}, \frac{1}{3}$

14. $\frac{8}{24}, \frac{4}{12}, \frac{2}{6}, \frac{1}{3}$

Page 104

1. $\frac{3}{8}$

2. $\frac{5}{12}$

3. $\frac{2}{6}$ or $\frac{1}{3}$

4. 30

5. 21

6. 5

7. 20

8. yes

9. no; Sample fractions: $\frac{1}{3}, \frac{2}{9}$

10. no; Sample fractions: $\frac{4}{10}; \frac{1}{3}$

11. yes

12. 18 questions

13. $2

14. You cannot tell. They may live in different houses that are the same distance from the store.

Page 105

1. $\frac{2}{6} < \frac{4}{6}$

2. $\frac{4}{5} > \frac{6}{10}$

3. $\frac{2}{4} = \frac{8}{16}$

4. <, like

5. =, unlike

6. <, like

7. >, like

8. <, unlike

9. >, unlike

10. $\frac{4}{10}, \frac{6}{10}, \frac{9}{10}$

11. $\frac{1}{6}, \frac{1}{2}, \frac{2}{3}, \frac{5}{6}$

12. Ming Lei

13. $\frac{1}{4}$

14. =

15. <

16. >

17. <

Page 106

1. <

2. <

3. <

4. <

5. >

6. >

7. <

8. <

9. >

10. >

11. <

12. >

13. <

14. <

15. >

16. Maria; Answers will vary. Possible answer: $\frac{1}{2} = \frac{2}{4} = \frac{4}{8}$, so $\frac{3}{8} < \frac{1}{2}$ and $\frac{3}{4}$ is $> \frac{1}{2}$.

17. Tyler

Page 107

1. =

2. <

3. <

4. >

5. <

6. =

7. >

8. =

9. >

10. =

11. >

12. >

13. pear trees

14. blueberries

15. $\frac{7}{8}$-qt bottle

16. Questions will vary.

Answers will vary for 17–22. Possible answers are given.

17. $\frac{3}{4}, \frac{5}{6}$

18. $\frac{7}{8}, \frac{10}{12}$

19. $\frac{2}{8}, \frac{3}{8}$

20. $\frac{4}{5}, \frac{9}{10}$

21. $\frac{3}{12}, \frac{4}{18}$

22. $\frac{15}{16}, \frac{31}{32}$

Page 108

1. <

2. <

3. >

4. >

5. >

6. >

7. <

8. >

9. <

10. >

11. >

12. <

13. >

14. =

15. =

16. >

17. $\frac{2}{15} < \frac{1}{5} < \frac{3}{5}$

18. $\frac{1}{8} < \frac{2}{3} < \frac{3}{4}$

19. $\frac{2}{5} < \frac{1}{2} < \frac{2}{3}$

20. $\frac{3}{8} < \frac{2}{3} < \frac{5}{6}$

21. $\frac{1}{3} < \frac{1}{2} < \frac{5}{9}$

22. $\frac{3}{12} < \frac{2}{6} < \frac{3}{4}$

23. Jesse

24. No; $\frac{3}{8} + \frac{5}{16} = \frac{11}{16}$

25. Possible answer: $\frac{7}{10}$

26. Possible answer: $\frac{7}{12}$

Page 109

1. $2\frac{4}{6}$ or $2\frac{2}{3}$

2. $1\frac{3}{8}$

3. $5\frac{1}{2}$

4. $5\frac{1}{2}$

5. $2\frac{1}{7}$

6. $1\frac{4}{8}$ or $1\frac{1}{2}$

7. $3\frac{1}{4}$

8. $3\frac{1}{3}$

9. $3\frac{2}{3}$ cups

10. $3\frac{1}{2}$ cans

11. $0.79

12. $3\frac{3}{4}$ cups

13. $2, 2\frac{1}{2}, 3, 3\frac{1}{2}$

14. $1\frac{2}{3}, 2, 2\frac{1}{3}, 2\frac{2}{3}$

15. $1\frac{6}{7}, 2\frac{2}{7}, 2\frac{5}{7}, 3\frac{1}{7}$

Page 110

1. $\frac{13}{5}$

2. $\frac{13}{3}$

3. $\frac{7}{5}$

4. $\frac{11}{3}$

5. $\frac{33}{8}$

6. $\frac{17}{10}$

7. $\frac{11}{2}$

8. $\frac{19}{8}$

9. $5\frac{1}{6}$

10. 2

11. $1\frac{7}{8}$

12. $2\frac{1}{6}$

13. $2\frac{3}{10}$

14. $3\frac{4}{5}$

15. $3\frac{2}{3}$

16. $4\frac{1}{2}$

17. She can measure out ten $\frac{1}{4}$-cup amounts of raisins because $\frac{10}{4} = 2\frac{2}{4}$.

18. thirteen $\frac{1}{4}$ cups

Page 111

1. $\frac{1}{5} + \frac{1}{5} + \frac{1}{5} + \frac{1}{5}$

2. $\frac{1}{8} + \frac{1}{8} + \frac{1}{8}$

3. $\frac{1}{12} + \frac{1}{12} + \frac{1}{12} + \frac{1}{12} + \frac{1}{12} + \frac{1}{12}$

4. $\frac{1}{4} + \frac{1}{4} + \frac{1}{4} + \frac{1}{4}$

Answers will vary for 5–6.

5. $\frac{7}{10} = \frac{2}{10} + \frac{3}{10} + \frac{2}{10}; \frac{7}{10} = \frac{4}{10} + \frac{2}{10} + \frac{1}{10}; \frac{7}{10} = \frac{5}{10} + \frac{1}{10} + \frac{1}{10}$

6. $\frac{6}{6} = \frac{4}{6} + \frac{1}{6} + \frac{1}{6}; \frac{6}{6} = \frac{2}{6} + \frac{2}{6} + \frac{2}{6};$

$\frac{6}{6} = \frac{3}{6} + \frac{2}{6} + \frac{1}{6}$

7. $\frac{1}{8}$ red, $\frac{1}{8}$ blue, $\frac{2}{8}$ green

8. $\frac{3}{6}$ blue, $\frac{2}{6}$ red, $\frac{1}{6}$ pink; $\frac{4}{6}$ blue, $\frac{1}{6}$ red, $\frac{1}{6}$ pink; $\frac{3}{6}$ blue, $\frac{1}{6}$ red, $\frac{2}{6}$ pink

Page 112

1. $5 \times \frac{1}{6}$

2. $7 \times \frac{1}{8}$

3. $5 \times \frac{1}{3}$

4. $9 \times \frac{1}{10}$

5. $3 \times \frac{1}{4}$

6. $11 \times \frac{1}{12}$

7. $4 \times \frac{1}{6}$

8. $8 \times \frac{1}{20}$

9. $13 \times \frac{1}{100}$

10. $\frac{2}{5}, \frac{3}{5}, \frac{4}{5}, \frac{5}{5}$

11. $\frac{2}{8}, \frac{3}{8}, \frac{4}{8}, \frac{5}{8}$

12. $\frac{1}{6}$ of the book

13. $\frac{1}{8}$ pound

Page 113

1. $\frac{6}{5}, \frac{9}{5}, \frac{12}{5}, \frac{15}{5}$

2. $\frac{4}{6}, \frac{6}{6}, \frac{8}{6}, \frac{10}{6}$

3. $\frac{8}{8}, \frac{12}{8}, \frac{16}{8}, \frac{20}{8}$

4. $\frac{10}{10}, \frac{15}{10}, \frac{20}{10}, \frac{25}{10}$

5. $8 \times \frac{1}{5}$

6. $10 \times \frac{1}{3}$

7. 6 times

8. 12 times

Page 114

1. $\frac{3}{6}$ or $\frac{1}{2}$

2. $\frac{9}{10}$

3. $\frac{3}{3}$ or 1

4. $\frac{3}{4}$

5. $\frac{6}{12}$ or $\frac{1}{2}$

6. $\frac{3}{6}$ or $\frac{1}{2}$

7. $\frac{12}{12}$ or 1

8. $\frac{7}{8}$

9. $\frac{4}{4}$ or 1

10. $\frac{3}{5}$

11. $\frac{9}{10}$ mi

12. $\frac{3}{8}$ of the pan

13. $\frac{3}{4}$ yd

14. $\frac{3}{3}$ lb or 1 lb

Page 115

1. $\frac{6}{8}$ or $\frac{3}{4}$

2. $\frac{2}{3}$

3. $\frac{5}{8}$

4. $\frac{9}{10}$

5. $\frac{5}{6}$

6. $\frac{3}{3}$ or 1

7. $\frac{3}{4}$

8. $\frac{7}{8}$

9. $\frac{4}{5}$

10. $\frac{8}{10}$ or $\frac{4}{5}$

11. $\frac{5}{8}$

12. $\frac{7}{12}$

13. $\frac{1}{5}$

14. $\frac{1}{3}$

15. $\frac{6}{10}$ or $\frac{3}{5}$

Page 116

1. $\frac{3}{5}$

2. $\frac{2}{4}$ or $\frac{1}{2}$

3. $\frac{4}{6}$ or $\frac{2}{3}$

4. $\frac{6}{8}$ or $\frac{3}{4}$

5. $\frac{1}{3}$

6. $\frac{6}{10}$ or $\frac{3}{5}$

7. $\frac{2}{4}$ or $\frac{1}{2}$

8. $\frac{2}{6}$ or $\frac{1}{3}$

9. $\frac{5}{8}$ lb

10. $\frac{2}{8}$ lb or $\frac{1}{4}$ lb

Page 117

1. $\frac{6}{9}$ or $\frac{2}{3}$

2. $\frac{1}{4}$

3. $\frac{5}{6}$

4. 1

5. 1

6. 1

7. 2

8. 5

9. 1

10. 7

11. 3

12. $\frac{5}{7}$

13. $\frac{6}{11}$

14. $\frac{3}{9}$ or $\frac{1}{3}$

15. $\frac{2}{5}$

16. $\frac{6}{12}$ or $\frac{1}{2}$

17. $\frac{4}{7}$

18. $\frac{1}{6}$ box

19. almost no orange juice left

20. $\frac{5}{12}$

Page 118

1. $\frac{12}{12}$ or 1

2. $\frac{2}{6}$ or $\frac{1}{3}$

3. $\frac{1}{5}$

4. $\frac{9}{10}$

5. $\frac{5}{8}$

6. $\frac{3}{4}$

7. $\frac{4}{12}$ or $\frac{1}{3}$

8. $\frac{3}{6}$ or $\frac{1}{2}$

9. $\frac{3}{3}$ or 1

10. $\frac{5}{10}$ mi or $\frac{1}{2}$ mi

11. $\frac{10}{10}$ mi or 1 mi

Page 119

1. $1 - \frac{3}{4} = \frac{1}{4}$ or $\frac{4}{4} - \frac{3}{4} = \frac{1}{4}$

2. $\frac{4}{8} + \frac{2}{8} = \frac{6}{8}$ or $\frac{3}{4}$

3. $\frac{2}{4} - \frac{1}{4} = \frac{1}{4}$

4. $\frac{7}{8}$

5. $\frac{4}{6}$ or $\frac{2}{3}$

6. $\frac{7}{8}$

7. $\frac{5}{10}$ or $\frac{1}{2}$

8. $\frac{3}{4}$

9. $\frac{3}{6}$ or $\frac{1}{2}$

10. $\frac{2}{5}$

11. $\frac{8}{10}$ or $\frac{4}{5}$

12. $\frac{5}{6}$

13. $\frac{4}{8}$ or $\frac{1}{2}$

14. 1 hr or $\frac{12}{12}$ hr

15. fourth grade

16. $\frac{5}{8}$

17. $\frac{5}{7}$

18. $\frac{9}{100}$

Page 120

1. false; $\frac{1}{2}$

2. true

3. false; $\frac{1}{2}$

4. false; $\frac{1}{3}$

5. $\frac{4}{5}$

6. $\frac{1}{2}$

7. $\frac{1}{6}$

8. $\frac{7}{8}$

9. $\frac{1}{3}$

10. $\frac{3}{4}$

11. $\frac{1}{4}$

12. $\frac{3}{10}$

13. $\frac{5}{10}$ mi or $\frac{1}{2}$ mi

14. $\frac{3}{8}$ tsp

15. a.

16. b.

17. a.

18. 16,520

19. 17,608

20. 28,294

21. 5,713

Page 121

1. $\frac{1}{2}$

2. $\frac{3}{5}$

3. 1

4. $\frac{4}{5}$

5. $1\frac{1}{5}$

6. $\frac{1}{3}$

7. $\frac{1}{2}$

8. $\frac{3}{4}$

9. $\frac{1}{5}$

10. $\frac{3}{5}$

11. $\frac{1}{3}$ yd

12. $1\frac{1}{2}$ in.

13. 35 instruments total

14. $\frac{10}{35} = \frac{2}{7}$. Possible explanation: This means that for every 7 instruments on display, 2 of them are guitars.

15. $\frac{25}{35}$ or $\frac{5}{7}$

Page 122

1. tenths

2. sixths

3. fourths

4. twelfths

5. tenths

6. eighths

7. $\frac{5}{6}$ of the lawn

8. 60 min; $\frac{1}{3} + \frac{2}{3} = \frac{3}{3} = 1$, and 1 hr = 60 min

Check work for 9–11.
Possible answers are given.

9. 6:00; either left or right side is shaded

10. 4:00; area between 12 and 4 is shaded

11. 9:00; area between 12 and 9 is shaded

Page 123

1. $3\frac{2}{8}$ or $3\frac{1}{4}$

2. $4\frac{7}{10}$

3. $6\frac{1}{6}$

4. $6\frac{2}{4}$ or $6\frac{1}{2}$

5. $4\frac{3}{4}$

6. $4\frac{4}{5}$

7. $2\frac{2}{6}$ or $2\frac{1}{3}$

8. $1\frac{7}{8}$ mi

9. $\frac{1}{8}$ mi longer

10. 8 times

Page 124

1. $13\frac{3}{5}$

2. $15\frac{1}{3}$

3. $7\frac{1}{5}$

4. $8\frac{2}{3}$

5. $2\frac{4}{8}$ or $2\frac{1}{2}$

6. $2\frac{4}{5}$

7. $1\frac{1}{6}$

8. $2\frac{5}{6}$

9. $3\frac{4}{5}$

10. $1\frac{3}{5}$

11. $1\frac{1}{2}$

12. $2\frac{3}{4}$

13. $5\frac{2}{3}$

167

14. $3\frac{4}{5}$

15. $4\frac{3}{10}$

16. $3\frac{1}{2}$ mi

17. $2\frac{1}{2}$ jars

18. $1\frac{3}{4}$, $1\frac{1}{2}$

19. $4\frac{2}{3}$, $4\frac{1}{3}$

Page 125

1. 8 children
2. Val
3. five 2-lb bags
4. 10 boards

Page 126

1. $\frac{10}{6}$ or $\frac{5}{3}$
2. $\frac{6}{5}$
3. $\frac{21}{10}$
4. $\frac{15}{12}$ or $\frac{5}{4}$
5. $\frac{18}{4}$ or $\frac{9}{2}$
6. $\frac{8}{8}$ or 1
7. $\frac{10}{3}$
8. $\frac{14}{8}$ or $\frac{7}{4}$
9. $\frac{24}{5}$
10. $\frac{25}{8}$ mi or $3\frac{1}{8}$ mi
11. $\frac{6}{3}$ c or 2 c

Page 127

1. $1\frac{1}{2}$
2. $1\frac{4}{5}$
3. $3\frac{3}{4}$
4. $4\frac{4}{5}$
5. $4\frac{2}{3}$
6. $5\frac{5}{6}$
7. $5\frac{3}{4}$
8. $12\frac{1}{4}$
9. $12\frac{4}{5}$
10. $4\frac{1}{2}$ hr
11. $10\frac{2}{3}$ c
12. rounded
13. rounded
14. exact
15. exact

Page 128

1. 5 ft
2. 7 mi
3. $2\frac{2}{3}$ lb
4. $\frac{4}{5}$ hr

Page 129

1. Check line plots.
   Table: $\frac{2}{6}$, 1 tally mark;
   $\frac{3}{6}$, 4 tally marks; $\frac{4}{6}$, 1 tally mark
2. 8 students
3. $\frac{3}{6}$ or $\frac{1}{2}$ hr
Check tally tables and line plots for 4–5.

Page 130

1. $\frac{1}{4}$
2. $\frac{1}{2}$
3. $\frac{1}{1}$ or 1
4. $\frac{1}{2}$ turn, counterclockwise
5. $\frac{3}{4}$ turn, clockwise
6. 1 full turn, counterclockwise.
7. $\frac{1}{4}$ turn clockwise, from 12 to 3
8. $\frac{1}{2}$ turn clockwise, from 12 to 6

Page 131

1. 0.7
2. 0.1
3. 0.4
4. 0.2
5. 0.5
6. 0.9
7. 0.3
8. $\frac{4}{10}$ or $\frac{2}{5}$
9. $\frac{8}{10}$ or $\frac{4}{5}$
10. $\frac{1}{10}$
11. $\frac{6}{10}$ or $\frac{3}{5}$
12. $\frac{6}{10}$ or $\frac{3}{5}$; 0.6
13. $\frac{3}{10}$; 0.3
14. 0.3, 0.2, 0.7, 0.5; 0.2, 0.3, 0.5, 0.7

Page 132

1. 0.20 or 0.2
2. 0.37
3. 0.83
4. 0.48
5. 0.09
6. $0.45

7. $0.62
8. 6
9. Ones place
10. 0.7, $0.70
11. $\frac{3}{10}$; 0.30 or 0.3
12. Dollars, Pennies

Page 133

1. 1.7
2. 3.5
3. 1.26
4. 6.7
5. 12.72
6. 27.04
7. $4\frac{3}{10}$
8. $9\frac{3}{100}$
9. $67\frac{29}{100}$
10. four and seven tenths
11. eight and ninety-two hundredths
12. $1.19
13. Jeff
14. Check drawings; Possible answer: If you could put the two grids on top of each other, the three shaded columns would match the 30 shaded small squares. They both represent the same part of the whole.

Page 134

Check standard notations for 1–3.

1. $5.55
2. $18.67
3. $14.79
4. c., $3.15
5. b., $40.21
6. no
7. yes

Page 135

1. $\frac{7}{10}$; 0.7
2. $\frac{64}{100}$ or $\frac{16}{25}$; 0.64
3. $2\frac{5}{10}$ or $2\frac{1}{2}$; 2.5
4. $1\frac{86}{100}$ or $1\frac{43}{50}$; 1.86
5. 12.3
6. 18.70 or 18.7
7. 0.02
8. 6.9
9. 16.2
10. 8.6
11. 10.99

168

12. $\frac{65}{100}$ or $\frac{13}{20}$
13. 26.07
14. $3\frac{1}{10}$
15. 3.3
16. $3\frac{5}{10}$
17. 3.7
18. $3\frac{9}{10}$

Page 136

1. <
2. >
3. >
4. <
5. >
6. <
7. =
8. <
9. 5.8, 5.62, 3.5, 0.46
10. 52.43, 52.41, 51.75, 51.7
11. Beatrice; Carmen
12. Joseph
13. 76.54
14. 45.67

Page 137

1. $\frac{50}{100}$, 0.50
2. $\frac{90}{100}$, 0.90
3. $\frac{20}{100}$, 0.20
4. $\frac{80}{100}$, 0.80
5. $\frac{4}{10}$, 0.4
6. $\frac{1}{10}$, 0.1
7. $\frac{6}{10}$, 0.6
8. $\frac{60}{100}$, 0.60
9. $\frac{8}{100}$

Page 138

1. $\frac{63}{100}$
2. $\frac{77}{100}$
3. $\frac{49}{100}$
4. $\frac{93}{100}$
5. $0.78
6. $0.59
7. $0.72
8. $\frac{78}{100}$ m or $\frac{39}{50}$ m
9. $\frac{69}{100}$ km

Page 139

Check work for 1–7.
1. triangle
2. circle
3. square
4. triangle
5. rectangle
6. triangle
7. rectangle

Page 140

Check work for 1–3.
Possible answers given.
1. The pattern is triangle, square, square; square, square, triangle.
2. The pattern is to add a column on the right with 1 more circle; 21 circles.
3. The pattern is 2 triangles placed base-to-base, 2 triangles placed vertex-to-vertex, 2 triangles placed vertex-to-vertex; Missing: 2 triangles placed vertex-to-vertex.

Page 141

Descriptions will vary for 1–5. Possible answers given.
1. 5, 13, 21, 29, 37, 45, 53, 61, 69, 77, 85, 93; All of the numbers in the pattern are odd.
2. 95, 88, 81, 74, 67, 60, 53, 46, 39, 32, 25, 18; The numbers alternate between odd and even.
3. 4, 19, 9, 24, 14, 29, 19, 34, 24, 39, 29, 44; The ones digit is always 4 or 9.
4. 2, 3, 6, 7, 14, 15, 30, 31, 62, 63, 126, 127; The numbers alternate between even and odd.
5. 1, 5, 9, 13, 17, 21, 25, 29; Rule: Add 4, First Term: 1
6. 11 tiles

Page 142

1. 17 min; 20 min
2. 16 pennies; 32 pennies
3. 4:23
4. 14; 18
5. Check drawings. The first two shapes should repeat.

Page 143

Check drawings for 1–4.
5. add 100
6. 98
7. add 20
8. 45, 60, 75
9. 800 + 50 + 6
10. 4,000 + 300 + 10 + 5
11. 66,702
12. 184,913

Page 144

1. Cathy, 8; Juanita, 6
2. noon, 6 min; after dinner, 9 min
3. fish book, $7; bird book, $9
4. 11 lionheads; 6 fantails
5. Jewel is first. Bill is last.
6. 7 chickens
7. Possible answer: Use what you learned from your guess to make a better guess. If the guess is too low, make a higher guess.

Page 145

Flowcharts may vary for 1–2.
1. $23
2. 2
3. 90 km
4. Peter
5. He ate dinner.
6. half past twelve or twelve thirty; 12:30
7. seven forty-eight or twelve min to eight; 7:48
8. nine twelve or twelve min after nine; 9:12

Page 146

1. 20 tomato plants; 5 bean plants
2. 4 hr in the afternoon; 2 hr after dinner
3. $7.01
4. $26
5. $43.95
6. $32
7. 70
8. 8,000
9. 10
10. 7,000
11. 20
12. 800
13. 75
14. 300
15. 7,000

169

Page 147

1. 8 gal
2. 40 min
3. 657 mi
4. 108 in.
5. $31
6. sparkle flashlight: 57¢; plain flashlight: 42¢
7. Check problems.

Page 148

1. mental math; 300 issues
2. calculator; $106.25
3. 65 different magazines
4. No
5. between business and news magazines
6. 5:55 A.M.
7. Check problems.

Page 149

1. 64 mi
2. $7.25
3. $669
4. 381 photos
5. 3:45 P.M.
6. 800 sq ft
7. 73 pesos
8. 19 pesos
9. 37 pesos

Page 150

1. 3 hr
2. $105
3. 1 hr 1 min or 61 minutes
4. $96
5. one 12-pack and four 16-packs
6. $1.99

Estimates may vary for 7–15.

7. 600
8. 200
9. 1,200
10. 3,600
11. 800
12. 900
13. 600
14. 700
15. 800

Page 151

Number sentences may vary for 1–2.

1. $40 + (40 - 10) + 72 = 142$ ft of pipe
2. $16 + 16 + 10 - 7 = \$35$
3. August
4. about 130 nails
5. $9
6. red, yellow, blue, green, white
7. Check problems.

Page 152

1. $565
2. Option 1
3. Option 2
4. Option 3

Answers will vary for 5–6.

7. 48 rolls
8. 28 lb; 50 lb
9. Check work.

Page 153

1. 9 rows; drop the remainder
2. 10 photos; remainder is the answer
3. 8 bags; round up
4. $2\frac{1}{4}$ oranges each; remainder is part of answer
5. $0.65
6. 14 minibuses
7. Check work.

170